STARTUPS ON A SHOESTRING

BOOTSTRAPPING YOUR WAY TO SUCCESS

NICK PERET

 BETTER BOSS

CONTENTS

~

To all aspiring tech entrepreneurs starting out on their amazing journeys,

May this book serve as a beacon of hope and inspiration as you navigate the exciting but challenging world of startups. May you find the courage and fortitude to overcome adversity, and may your passion and determination lead you to the success you deserve.

This book is written in your honor.

ACKNOWLEDGMENTS

～

Writing this book has been an incredible journey, and many people have provided invaluable assistance, guidance, and encouragement. I am grateful to each and every one of you.

First and foremost, I want to express my heartfelt appreciation to my previous business partners and mentors. Your wisdom, experience, and camaraderie have been invaluable to my development as an entrepreneur, and I am grateful for the opportunity to learn from and collaborate with you.

Thank you to my current advisors for your unwavering support and for pushing me to think bigger and achieve more. Your expertise and insights have been invaluable in shaping this book and my overall entrepreneurial journey.

Brittney, my wonderful fiancée, I cannot thank you enough for your love, patience, and understanding. Throughout the long nights and weekends spent working on this book, you have been my rock, and your faith in me has been a constant source of strength and motivation.

I will be eternally grateful to the clients who trusted me and let me be a part of their success stories. Your trust and collaboration not only influenced the content of this book but also shaped my approach to business and life.

Last but not least, I'd like to express my heartfelt gratitude to my parents. Your unwavering love, support, and encouragement have helped me succeed, and I will be eternally grateful for the values and work ethic you instilled in me at a young age.

Thank you for being a part of my journey and helping to make this book a reality.

Copyright Page

Copyright © 2023 by Nick Peret

For permission requests, write to the publisher at the address below:

Better Boss Brands Co.

Denver, CO 80209

Nick@betterboss.io

Cover design by Nick Peret

Book layout and design by Nick Peret

ISBN: 979-8387583230

Printed in the United States of America

First Edition: March 2023

❀ Created with Vellum

PREFACE

~

The road to entrepreneurship is both exciting and difficult. It is full of obstacles, late nights, and moments of doubt. It does, however, bring with it the possibility of extraordinary personal growth, self-discovery, and the opportunity to make a meaningful impact on the world around us. I understand the rollercoaster ride that is entrepreneurship as an entrepreneur who has experienced the highs and lows of building businesses from the ground up.

Throughout my years in the tech and startup industries, I've seen the importance of innovation, adaptability, and resource-fulness grow. Time and again, I've seen how the ability to bootstrap a business and make the most of limited resources can mean the difference between success and failure. In this book, I hope to share the insights, strategies, and lessons I've learned along the way in my own entrepreneurial journey, with a particular emphasis on the art of bootstrapping a tech startup.

"Startups on a Shoestring: Bootstrapping Your Way to Success" is a hands-on guide that will help aspiring tech entrepreneurs navigate the often perplexing world of startups. I poured my heart and soul into this book, not only sharing my own experiences but also the stories of others who have successfully bootstrapped their businesses.

As you read through these pages, I hope you find the information, inspiration, and motivation you need to face and overcome the challenges that lie ahead. This book is about cultivating a mindset of resilience, resourcefulness, and determination that will serve you well throughout your entrepreneurial journey, not just the nuts and bolts of building a bootstrapped startup.

I am honored to be a part of your journey and am looking forward to seeing what amazing things you will accomplish as you take your first steps into the world of tech entrepreneurship. Best wishes for your success!

INTRODUCTION

∼

Starting a business in today's fast-paced, ever-changing world of technology and innovation can be both exciting and intimidating. With countless success stories of tech startups making headlines and changing the landscape of various industries, it's no surprise that many aspiring entrepreneurs want to start their own businesses. The harsh reality is that a significant number of startups fail within their first few years of operation, often due to a lack of resources, a lack of experience, and an inability to navigate the numerous challenges that come with starting a business from scratch.

"Startups on a Shoestring: Bootstrapping Your Way to Success" is a comprehensive guide designed to assist aspiring tech entrepreneurs in overcoming these challenges and building successful businesses on a shoestring budget. This book aims to equip you with the tools, strategies, and mindset needed to navigate the complex world of bootstrapping, allowing you to make the most of every dollar and resource at your disposal.

This book covers a wide range of topics critical to the success of your bootstrapped venture, drawing on my own experiences in the tech and startup space as well as the stories of other successful bootstrapped entrepreneurs. Each chapter offers practical advice, real-world examples, and valuable insights that will help you build a strong foundation for your business, from validating your business idea and crafting a lean business plan to mastering sales and customer acquisition.

Throughout the book, you will learn the value of resourcefulness, creativity, and perseverance, as well as how to cultivate a resilient mindset that will allow you to overcome the inevitable challenges and setbacks along the way. My hope is that by sharing the lessons I've learned on my own entrepreneurial journey as well as the journeys of others who have successfully bootstrapped their startups, you will feel inspired and empowered to take on the challenges of building your own tech startup on a shoestring budget.

I encourage you to keep an open mind as you read this book and to remember that the road to success is rarely a straight path. It is my sincere hope that the insights, strategies, and stories shared within these pages will not only provide you with the necessary knowledge and tools for success, but will also inspire you to embrace the journey ahead with passion, determination, and unwavering resilience.

Hello and welcome to the world of bootstrapped technology startups. Your path to success begins right here.

INTRODUCTION TO BOOTSTRAPPING

≈

As I sat in bumper-to-bumper traffic, inching towards the office where I would spend the next eight hours making cold calls, the morning sun glared through my windshield. In the high-stakes world of tech startup sales, it was just another day. But, as I gripped the steering wheel in frustration, I couldn't shake the feeling that there had to be more to life than this daily grind. I needed to make a change.

I dialed a friend's number and informed him that I was quitting my job. I had no concrete plan in place, only a burning desire to break free from the confines of the 9-to-5 grind. I asked him if he would assist me with my personal expenses if I ran out of money while attempting to build my own thing. He agreed, much to my relief.

I embarked on the journey of bootstrapping my first company with a meager budget and no clear roadmap. I lived on $1,500 per month for the first six months, learning to be resourceful and resilient as I navigated the uncharted waters of entrepreneurship.

Bootstrapping my startup was not only a necessity; it was

also a conscious decision. With few resources and no outside funding, bootstrapping forced me to be resourceful and make the most of what I had. I quickly realized that this approach to entrepreneurship would not only put my resolve to the test, but would also lead to enormous personal growth.

Bootstrapping was my only option at the time, and I'm grateful for it now. If I had relied on outside funding, I might have missed out on some of the most valuable lessons that came from starting a business from the ground up. As a boot-strapped entrepreneur, the constraints I faced forced me to think creatively, solve problems in unconventional ways, and truly understand the value of every dollar spent.

The accelerated learning curve was one of the most signifi-cant advantages of bootstrapping. I had to wear many hats and quickly adapt to new situations because there was no safety net or external support. I gained hands-on experience in every aspect of running a business, from marketing and sales to product development and customer service. This not only gave me a well-rounded skill set, but it also gave me a deep appreci-ation for the challenges and triumphs of entrepreneurship.

As I continued to bootstrap my startup, I realized the value of personal development. Building a business with limited resources required a great deal of dedication, resilience, and self-belief. I encountered numerous setbacks and obstacles, but with each one, I learned more about myself and what I was capable of accomplishing.

The sense of control and ownership that comes with boot-strapping can be extremely empowering. I had the freedom to make my own decisions and shape the direction of my company because I had no external investors to answer to. This independence enabled me to stay true to my vision and build a company that truly reflected my values and passions.

In retrospect, the bootstrapping journey was a transforma-tive experience that shaped not only my startup but also forged me into a stronger, more resilient entrepreneur. The lessons I learned along the way continue to serve me well in my current endeavors, and I am grateful for the opportunities for growth, knowledge, and self-discovery that bootstrapping has provided in my life.

Defining Bootstrapping

In the context of entrepreneurship, bootstrapping refers to the process of starting and growing a business with little to no external funding, relying primarily on personal savings, company revenue, and other creative ways to stretch resources. The term "bootstrapping" comes from the phrase "pulling oneself up by one's bootstraps," which implies that entrepreneurs who choose this path are self-sufficient and resourceful in their business development.

To make the most of their limited resources, entrepreneurs can use one of several bootstrapping strategies:

- **Personal savings:** Entrepreneurs can use their personal savings to fund the early stages of their businesses. Money from their regular jobs, investments, or even loans from friends and family can all be used to fund this.

- **Pre-sales or advance payments:** By offering a product or service for pre-sale, entrepreneurs can generate revenue before the product is actually available, assisting in the development and production of the product.

- **Entrepreneurs can use bartering and trading** to acquire resources without spending money by exchanging goods or services with other businesses or individuals.

- **Entrepreneurs can save money** on hiring professionals by handling multiple aspects of their business themselves. Marketing, design, and administration are examples of such tasks.

- **Running a business with low overhead** and focusing on essential costs can help entrepreneurs save money and allocate it more strategically.

- **Crowdfunding:** Crowdfunding platforms such as Kickstarter and Indiegogo enable entrepreneurs to raise funds from a large number of people in exchange for rewards or equity in the company.

- **Grants and competitions:** Entering business competitions or applying for grants can provide entrepreneurs with the funds they need to grow their businesses without sacrificing equity or incurring debt.

Bootstrapping a business strategically necessitates careful planning and prioritization. Entrepreneurs should:

- *Create a solid business plan* outlining their objectives, strategies, and financial projections.

- *Make a budget* that accounts for necessary expenses and identifies areas where expenses can be reduced.

- *Concentrate on generating revenue* as soon as possible in order to fund ongoing operations and growth.

- They must ***constantly evaluate and adjust their strategies*** in order to make the best use of available resources.

- ***Maintain your flexibility*** and adapt to changing market conditions and opportunities.

Entrepreneurs can build successful businesses with limited resources while maintaining control and ownership of their ventures by employing these bootstrapping strategies and staying focused on their goals.

Advantages of Bootstrapping

For entrepreneurs willing to take on the challenge, adopting the bootstrapping mindset can provide several benefits. While it may not be the most straightforward path, the benefits can far outweigh the challenges, making it an appealing option for many business owners. Some of the primary benefits of bootstrapping include:

- **Control:** When entrepreneurs bootstrap their businesses, they retain complete ownership and control over their enterprises. This means they can make decisions based on their vision and values without having to answer to outside investors or stakeholders with competing priorities.

- **Fostering creativity:** Due to limited resources, bootstrapped entrepreneurs are frequently forced to think outside the box and devise innovative solutions to problems. This can lead to the creation of novel products, services, and business models that distinguish their companies from the competition.

- **Customers must be prioritized:** Because bootstrapped businesses rely on customer revenue to fund their operations, they must be laser-focused on understanding and meeting their customers' needs. This customer-focused approach can assist entrepreneurs in developing strong relationships and cultivating brand loyalty.

- Bootstrapping *teaches entrepreneurs to be financially prudent* and to make the most of their limited resources. As the business grows, this discipline can translate into better financial management practices, ensuring long-term stability and success.

- **Faster path to profitability:** Because bootstrapped businesses must generate revenue quickly in order to survive, they tend to prioritize profitability over companies that have access to external funding. This can lay a solid financial foundation for future expansion.

- **Greater adaptability:** Because there are fewer stakeholders to answer to, bootstrapped entrepreneurs can more easily pivot and adapt their businesses in response to market changes or new opportunities.

- **Personal and professional development:** The challenges and risks of bootstrapping can help entrepreneurs develop critical skills and resilience that will serve them well throughout their careers.

- **Higher valuation:** By not seeking outside funding, bootstrapped businesses can establish a track

record of success and profitability, which can lead
to a higher valuation in the event of an acquisition
or future fundraising round.

The bootstrapping journey may be difficult, but it allows
entrepreneurs to shape their businesses according to their
vision and values, while also encouraging creativity and innovation. Bootstrapped entrepreneurs can build successful,
long-lasting businesses by focusing on their customers and
maintaining control over their businesses.

Disadvantages of Bootstrapping

While there are numerous benefits to bootstrapping, it is
important to recognize that this approach also has its challenges and drawbacks. Understanding these potential disadvantages can assist entrepreneurs in making informed
decisions about whether bootstrapping is the best path for
their businesses. Some of the significant disadvantages of
bootstrapping are as follows:

- **Slower growth:** Bootstrapping businesses typically
  grow at a slower rate than those that have access to
  external funding. This is primarily due to the fact
  that they must rely solely on profits to reinvest in
  expansion initiatives, which can limit the scope and
  speed of expansion.

- **Limited resources:** Entrepreneurs who choose to
  bootstrap their businesses may face financial and
  personnel constraints. This can sometimes result in
  increased workload and stress, as well as
  difficulties attracting top talent in the absence of the
  allure of generous salaries and benefits.

- **Increased risk:** Taking on personal financial risk when bootstrapping a business is common. Entrepreneurs may need to invest their personal savings or use personal credit to fund their operations, which can jeopardize their personal financial stability.

- **Limited networking opportunities:** Small businesses that are bootstrapped may miss out on valuable connections and networking opportunities that can come from working with investors or participating in accelerator programs.

- Entrepreneurs who bootstrap their businesses *may not have access to the same level of expertise and mentorship* that can be obtained by partnering with experienced investors or advisors.

- **Burnout risk:** The demands of bootstrapping, such as long hours, financial stress, and a seemingly never-ending list of responsibilities, can wear on entrepreneurs, leading to burnout and potential harm to their mental and physical well-being.

- **Difficulties with scaling:** Without significant outside funding, bootstrapped businesses may struggle to scale their operations quickly enough to keep up with market demands or capitalize on time-sensitive opportunities.

Despite these obstacles, many entrepreneurs choose to bootstrap their businesses in order to overcome them and build successful, self-sustaining businesses. Before embarking on this journey, entrepreneurs must carefully weigh the pros and cons of bootstrapping, as well as develop strategies to address any challenges that may arise.

Famous Bootstrapped Success Stories

The world of entrepreneurship is full of inspiring stories about successful bootstrapped businesses that defied the odds and achieved incredible success. These stories not only inspire aspiring entrepreneurs but also teach them valuable lessons that they can apply to their own journeys. Consider two well-known bootstrapped success stories:

MailChimp was founded in 2001 by Ben Chestnut and Dan Kurzius as a small email marketing service with no outside funding. The founders were determined to create a user-friendly platform with a quirky brand personality that would appeal to small businesses. MailChimp has grown organically over the years, reinvesting profits to fuel its expansion. It is now one of the world's leading email marketing platforms, with millions of users and over $700 million in annual revenue.

The following are the most important takeaways from MailChimp's journey:

- Concentrate on *developing a distinct brand identity* that speaks to your target audience.

- *Prioritize customer needs* and improve your product in response to their feedback.

- *Allow your business to grow organically* over time by being patient and persistent.

Basecamp was founded in 2004 by Jason Fried and David Heinemeier Hansson as a simple project management tool to address the founders' own collaboration challenges. With no outside funding, the duo relied on their design and programming expertise to create a product that drew a loyal customer base. Basecamp is now used by millions of people worldwide and generates tens of millions of dollars in revenue each year.

The following are the most important takeaways from Basecamp's journey:

- *Solve a real-world problem* that you understand and care about.

- *Make the most of your distinct skills* and expertise to create a standout product.

- *Focus on retaining customers* by consistently providing value and excellent customer service.

These stories demonstrate that it is possible to build a successful business through bootstrapping with determination, creativity, and a relentless focus on delivering value to customers. Aspiring entrepreneurs can take lessons from these examples and apply them to their own ventures, charting their own course to bootstrapped success.

Bootstrapping vs. Fundraising

As we've seen, bootstrapping can result in amazing success stories. However, it is critical to understand that this is not the only way to build a successful business. Raising external funds through methods such as venture capital and angel investing may be a better fit for many entrepreneurs. Let's compare bootstrapping to these other funding options to help you decide which is best for your startup.

Bootstrapping

- You *retain complete control and ownership* of your company.

- *Financial resources are limited,* which often leads to slower growth.

- You are *free to make decisions* without being pressured by investors.

- It *encourages creativity and resourcefulness* because you must make the most of the available resources.

It may not be appropriate for startups that require substantial upfront capital investment.

Venture Capital (VC)

- Provides significant *funding to accelerate growth.*

- *Investors typically take equity in your company* and have the ability to influence decision-making.

- Connections to *influential networks and experienced mentors* can aid in the development of your startup.

- The *emphasis is frequently on rapid growth and scaling,* which can put founders under pressure.

- It may be a *better fit for startups with high growth potential* and a clear path to profitability.

Angel Investing

- Individual *investors with industry experience* typically provide funding.

- Angel investors *may take equity in your company*, but they are typically less involved than venture capitalists.

- Based on their expertise, they can provide *valuable mentorship* and connections.

- The amount of *funding is typically less than that of venture capital*, but it can assist startups in growing at a more manageable pace.

- It may be *appropriate for early-stage startups* looking for advice and financial support from experienced entrepreneurs.

Each funding option has its own set of benefits and drawbacks, and the best option is determined by factors such as your business model, growth potential, and personal preferences. As an entrepreneur, you must carefully weigh your options and choose the path that best fits your vision, values, and long-term goals. Whether you choose to bootstrap or seek outside funding, keep in mind that success is built on perseverance, adaptability, and a relentless focus on providing value to your customers.

The Entrepreneurial Spirit

The decision to bootstrap a business is frequently motivated by a deep entrepreneurial spirit that drives founders to take complete control of their destiny. This spirit is distinguished by traits such as determination, resilience, and unwavering faith in one's vision. Let's look at the mindset and characteristics of entrepreneurs who choose to bootstrap their businesses and how this approach can shape the very foundation of their businesses.

- **Self-sufficiency:** Bootstrapping entrepreneurs are resourceful and skilled at solving problems without relying on outside funding. This self-reliance allows them to overcome obstacles and quickly adapt to changing circumstances.

- **Financial discipline:** Bootstrapped entrepreneurs learn to carefully manage their finances, prioritizing necessary expenses and making wise investments to fuel growth. This financial prudence frequently results in a more sustainable and profitable business model.

- Limited resources frequently *force bootstrapping entrepreneurs to think outside the box,* devising innovative solutions and ideas to differentiate themselves in the market.

- **Risk-taking:** To bootstrap a startup, you must be willing to take risks and face the unknown. Entrepreneurs who take on this challenge gain a strong sense of self-belief and confidence in their ability to overcome adversity.

- **Customer-centricity:** Entrepreneurs who are bootstrapping understand that their success is dependent on providing value to their customers. They remain focused on meeting the needs of customers, developing strong relationships, and ensuring customer satisfaction.

- **Agility and adaptability:** Because they lack the bureaucracy and investor pressures that larger, funded companies may face, bootstrapped startups are often more nimble and responsive to market changes. Because of their adaptability, they can pivot and evolve as needed.

- **Long-term vision:** Bootstrapping entrepreneurs have a long-term vision and are willing to make short-term sacrifices to achieve their goals. They understand that it takes time, patience, and persistence to build a successful business.

The challenges of bootstrapping necessitate unwavering passion and commitment to the business. This passion fuels the motivation to persevere in the face of adversity and remain focused on the ultimate goal of success.

When entrepreneurs embrace the bootstrapping mindset and these characteristics, they shape the foundation of their startups, often resulting in a more resilient, innovative, and customer-focused business. The lessons learned through bootstrapping not only contribute to the startup's success but also play an important role in the entrepreneurs' personal and professional development.

Setting Realistic Expectations

As we delve into the world of bootstrapping, it's critical to establish realistic expectations for the journey ahead. While the potential rewards are significant, the road to success is frequently paved with challenges and risks that entrepreneurs must be prepared to face. You'll be better equipped to navigate the ups and downs of entrepreneurship and make informed decisions if you know what to expect when bootstrapping a startup.

- **Time commitment:** Because founders frequently wear multiple hats and handle various aspects of the business, bootstrapping a startup necessitates a significant time investment. Be prepared to work long hours and make personal sacrifices in order for your venture to succeed.

- **Financial difficulties:** As a bootstrapped entrepreneur, you will most likely face financial constraints and will be responsible for carefully managing cash flow. You may need to make difficult decisions about how to allocate limited resources and come up with innovative ways to stretch your budget.

- **Slow growth:** Without external funding, your company may grow at a slower rate than startups that receive significant investments. This can be frustrating, but it is critical to remain patient and focused on long-term growth.

- Bootstrapping a startup *can be an emotional rollercoaster* filled with highs and lows. Be prepared to face setbacks, self-doubt, and challenges, as well as to celebrate your accomplishments and milestones.

- **Learning curve:** As a bootstrapped entrepreneur, you will almost certainly need to learn new skills and knowledge in various areas of your business. This can be exciting as well as overwhelming, but it is critical to embrace the learning process and grow as a founder.

- **Failure risk:** As with any business venture, there is always the possibility of failure when bootstrapping a startup. It is critical to understand and accept this risk, as well as to learn from mistakes and remain resilient in the face of adversity.

- Despite the challenges and risks, *the rewards of successfully bootstrapping a startup can be enormous*. These include keeping control of your business, reaping the financial rewards of your efforts, and experiencing the satisfaction of creating something from the ground up.

You'll be better prepared to embark on this entrepreneurial journey if you set realistic expectations and understand the challenges and potential rewards of bootstrapping a startup. Accept the learning opportunities that come your way, stay focused on your goals, and remember that perseverance and resilience are essential for overcoming obstacles and achieving success.

Bootstrapping in the Tech Industry

The technology industry is a dynamic, rapidly changing landscape that offers unique opportunities and challenges to bootstrapped entrepreneurs. The principles of bootstrapping can be especially beneficial in this exciting environment, allowing founders to adapt quickly and stay ahead of the competition. Let us look at some of the reasons why bootstrapping is ideal for technology startups:

- **Lean development:** Companies that can develop and launch innovative products quickly are frequently rewarded in the tech industry.

Bootstrapping promotes lean development, in which startups create minimum viable products (MVPs) and iterate based on customer feedback. This approach enables tech startups to remain agile and more effectively respond to market demands.

- Affordable and *powerful software development tools, cloud services, and open-source resources have made it easier than ever* for bootstrapped tech startups to build and scale their products without breaking the bank.

- **Remote work and global talent:** With the widespread adoption of remote work, bootstrapped tech startups can tap into a global talent pool and build diverse, high-performing teams without the need for costly office space or relocation costs.

- Due to the inherent scalability of digital products and services, *tech startups often have the potential to scale quickly and achieve significant growth*. Startups that can efficiently tap into this potential may see exponential growth and success.

- **Early revenue generation:** Unlike in other industries, tech startups can often generate revenue relatively quickly by launching paid products, offering subscription services, or implementing other monetization strategies. This can provide cash flow to bootstrapped startups in order to sustain and grow their businesses.

- **Culture of innovation:** The tech industry thrives on disruption and innovation, which aligns well with the bootstrapping mindset. Entrepreneurs motivated by passion and creativity can use bootstrapping principles to create game-changing products and services that challenge the status quo.

- Bootstrapping provides entrepreneurs with a *viable path to success in the fast-paced world of technology startups by enabling lean development*, cost-effective scaling, and rapid growth. Founders can position themselves to create innovative solutions that have a long-term impact by embracing the challenges and opportunities that come with bootstrapping in the tech industry.

Preparing for the Bootstrapping Journey

Bootstrapping can be both exciting and difficult, requiring entrepreneurs to mentally and financially prepare for the road ahead. Founders can successfully navigate the complexities of bootstrapping a startup by arming themselves with the right mindset, resources, and strategies.

Here are some pointers to help entrepreneurs prepare for their venture into bootstrapping:

- **Develop a resilient mindset:** Accept that challenges and setbacks are unavoidable, and cultivate the mental fortitude to overcome them. Adopt a growth mindset and see every challenge as an opportunity to learn and grow.

- **Establish clear objectives and priorities:** Set realistic goals and expectations for the growth and development of your startup. Prioritize tasks and allocate resources wisely to make steady progress toward these objectives.

- **Create a thorough financial plan:** Make a detailed budget outlining your startup's projected expenses and revenue. Identify areas where you can save money or improve efficiency, and be ready to adjust your financial plan as your circumstances change.

- **Create a strong support network:** Surround yourself with mentors, peers, and advisors who can provide guidance, support, and encouragement as you face the challenges of bootstrapping. Attend networking events, join online communities, and look for ways to connect with other entrepreneurs.

- **Learn to be resourceful:** Bootstrapping necessitates making the best use of limited resources. Develop the skills and knowledge required to identify creative solutions and workarounds, whether it's locating cost-effective tools, negotiating better deals with suppliers, or utilizing your personal network for assistance.

- *Maintain a close relationship with your customers* and prioritize their needs. This focus will assist you in developing products and services that will appeal to your target audience and generate the revenue required to sustain and grow your startup.

- **Educate yourself on a regular basis:** Keep up to date on industry trends, best practices, and emerging technologies that may have an impact on your startup. To stay agile and competitive in your market, invest time in learning new skills and expanding your knowledge base.

- **Make a long-term plan:** bootstrapping is a marathon, not a sprint. Prepare to put a significant amount of time and effort into your startup, as well as the patience and perseverance required to see it through to success.

Entrepreneurs can set themselves up for success and better navigate the challenges that lie ahead by mentally and financially preparing for the bootstrapping journey. Founders can overcome obstacles and build thriving, sustainable startups with a resilient mindset, clear goals, and the right support network.

The Role of Passion and Persistence

As we conclude this primer on bootstrapping, it's critical to emphasize the importance of passion and perseverance in the success of bootstrapped entrepreneurs. Building a business from the ground up with limited resources and no outside funding can be a daunting and difficult task. However, it is your passion for your idea and your unwavering persistence in the face of obstacles that will ultimately determine success or failure.

Even during the most difficult times, entrepreneurs are motivated and energized by their passion. It is your passion for your product, service, or mission that drives your desire to innovate and create value for your customers. When you're enthusiastic about your startup, you'll be more willing to put in the time, effort, and money to see it succeed.

Persistence, on the other hand, is the ability to keep going even when the odds appear to be stacked against you. As a bootstrapped entrepreneur, you will almost certainly face a slew of setbacks, challenges, and roadblocks. To overcome these obstacles and achieve your goals, you must be able to persevere, learn from your mistakes, and adapt your approach.

Passion and persistence combine to form a potent combination that enables bootstrapped entrepreneurs to overcome obstacles and build successful, long-term businesses. As you embark on your own bootstrapping journey, keep your passion for your idea alive and cultivate the perseverance required to see it through to completion.

With the basics of bootstrapping established, it's time to delve deeper into the mindset and strategies that will aid you in your entrepreneurial endeavor. We'll look at "The Bootstrapper's Mindset" in the next chapter, delving into the attitudes, beliefs, and behaviors that can help you thrive as a bootstrapped entrepreneur.

2

THE BOOTSTRAPPER'S MINDSET

～

I recall picking up my first batch of business cards, which bore the title "CEO" beneath my name. I couldn't shake the feeling of being an imposter as I clutched the cards in my hand, despite being only 25 years old. The burden of responsibility weighed heavily on my shoulders, and I wondered if I had what it took to run a business.

Months later, I was sprinting to the bank, my heart pounding in my chest as I transferred my personal funds into the company account. I was desperate to make payroll, afraid that my team would lose trust in me as their leader if I didn't. I felt like a fraud in those moments, questioning my decision to become an entrepreneur.

However, as time went on, I learned how to navigate the challenges of bootstrapping a startup. I developed into a self-assured entrepreneur, adopting a mindset that allowed me to face challenges head-on and cultivate a presence that made me feel like I could accomplish anything. This transformation was no accident – it was the result of adopting a bootstrapper's mindset.

Bootstrapped entrepreneurs must cultivate a mindset focused on resourcefulness, creativity, and perseverance. Understanding and implementing these mindset principles will better equip you to navigate the rollercoaster journey of bootstrapping a startup and emerge as a confident, capable entrepreneur capable of turning challenges into opportunities for growth and success.

Resourcefulness, Creativity, and Perseverance

A mindset centered on resourcefulness, creativity, and perseverance is critical in the world of bootstrapped startups. Limited resources and the lack of external funding frequently force entrepreneurs to think outside the box, devising creative solutions to overcome obstacles and turn them into opportunities.

As a bootstrapped entrepreneur, you'll frequently have to make the most of what you have and stretch your resources as far as possible. This entails constantly looking for cost-effective solutions, making strategic decisions, and figuring out how to cut costs without sacrificing quality. To develop resourcefulness, you must be open-minded, adaptable, and willing to try new approaches to problem-solving.

Creativity is required when bootstrapping because entrepreneurs must find unique solutions to overcome obstacles and differentiate themselves from competitors. This can include creating new products or services, devising clever marketing strategies, or discovering new ways to connect with customers. To embrace creativity, you must be willing to take risks, challenge the status quo, and learn from both successes and failures.

The bootstrapping journey can be difficult, and it's critical to remain determined and persistent in the face of setbacks and challenges. Perseverance entails sticking to your vision even when things get tough, as well as being willing to learn from mistakes and adapt your approach as needed. You must develop resilience, grit, and an unwavering belief in your ability to succeed in order to cultivate perseverance.

You'll be better equipped to navigate the complex world of bootstrapped startups and maximize your chances of success if you focus on these three key components.

Overcoming Common Mental Barriers and Challenges

As a bootstrapped entrepreneur, the road to success is frequently paved with mental barriers and challenges that can frustrate your progress. By recognizing and addressing these challenges, you can build the resilience and strength needed to persevere and achieve your goals.

Here are common mental barriers & how to overcome them:

- **Fear of Failure:** Many entrepreneurs, particularly those who are bootstrapping, are afraid that their venture will fail. Reframe your mindset to view failure as an opportunity for learning and growth to overcome this fear. Accept the idea that setbacks can provide valuable insights that will help you succeed in the long run.

- **Imposter Syndrome:** It's not uncommon for bootstrapped entrepreneurs to feel like frauds or that their accomplishments are undeserved. Remind yourself of your accomplishments, skills, and hard work to combat imposter syndrome. Surround yourself with people who believe in your abilities and can provide encouragement when you need it.

- **Burnout:** The physical and mental exhaustion that comes with bootstrapping can be severe. Prioritize self-care and maintain a healthy work-life balance to avoid burnout. Establish boundaries, take breaks, and make time for relaxation and hobbies outside of work.

- **Perfectionism:** Pursuing perfection can stymie progress and lead to procrastination. Accept that perfection is an unattainable goal and instead concentrate on incremental improvements. Set reasonable expectations and deadlines, and don't be afraid to release your product or service even if it isn't perfect - you can always iterate and improve over time.

- **Isolation:** Because bootstrapped entrepreneurs frequently work alone or in small groups, they may experience feelings of isolation. To stay connected and gain valuable insights from others facing similar challenges, seek out networking opportunities, join entrepreneur communities, and maintain open communication with friends and family.

By identifying and addressing these mental roadblocks, you will be better prepared to overcome the challenges you will face on your bootstrapping journey. You'll find it easier to stay focused, motivated, and determined in the face of adversity as your mental resilience grows.

Adopting a Lean Approach

Every dollar counts in a bootstrapped startup, and efficiency is essential. Adopting a lean mindset can assist you in making better decisions, maximizing your limited resources, and ultimately increasing your chances of success.

Let's look at the key elements of a lean mindset and how they apply to bootstrapped businesses:

- **Resource Efficiency:** For bootstrapped entrepreneurs, being mindful of your resources is critical. Concentrate on making the best use of your available resources, whether they are money, time, or talent. Identify areas where you can cut costs without sacrificing quality, and look for ways to streamline your processes and eliminate waste on a regular basis.

- **Prioritization:** Because resources are limited, it is critical to prioritize tasks and projects that have the greatest impact on your business. Create a system for assessing the importance and urgency of tasks, and focus your efforts on those that will add the most value to your startup.

- **Effective Decision-Making:** Under pressure, bootstrapped entrepreneurs must be decisive and make difficult decisions. Develop a mindset that values data-driven decision-making and is willing to pivot when necessary. Learn from your mistakes, and don't be afraid to pivot if your initial strategy isn't producing the desired results.

- Adopting *a lean mindset entails constantly looking for ways to improve and optimize your business*. Evaluate your processes, products, and services on a regular basis, and actively seek feedback from customers and team members.

Utilize this feedback to make data-driven improvements and ensure that you are always progressing.

- **Minimum Viable Product (MVP):** It is critical in a bootstrapped startup to focus on launching a minimum viable product as soon as possible. This allows you to test your idea in the market, collect valuable feedback, and iterate on your product without investing a lot of time and money upfront. Accept the concept of "failing fast" in order to learn and adapt quickly.

You'll be better equipped to navigate the challenges of bootstrapping and make the most of your limited resources if you adopt a lean mindset. You'll lay a stronger foundation for your startup's success if you prioritize efficiency, prioritization, and continuous improvement.

The Power of Patience

Bootstrapped entrepreneurs frequently experience slower growth than their counterparts who receive external funding. While venture-backed startups have the resources to scale quickly, bootstrapped startups must rely on organic growth and revenue generation. As a result, bootstrapped entrepreneurs must cultivate patience throughout their journey.

- **Accept the Slow Burn:** While bootstrapped startups may take longer to reach significant milestones, the slower pace can be beneficial. By focusing on consistent, long-term growth, you can lay a solid foundation for your company and avoid the pitfalls of rapid expansion. Remind yourself that success is a marathon, not a sprint and that every step forward counts.

- **Set Realistic Expectations:** As a bootstrapped entrepreneur, it's critical to understand your growth potential and the time it may take to achieve your objectives. Be prepared to adjust your expectations and timelines as needed, and keep in mind that progress may be slower than you anticipated.

- **Celebrate Small Wins:** In a bootstrapped startup, every accomplishment, no matter how small, is significant. Celebrate each milestone, and use these small victories to keep you motivated and focused on the big picture.

- **Cultivate Resilience:** Patience and resilience go hand in hand. There will be setbacks and challenges along the way, and developing the mental fortitude to weather these storms is critical. Accept the learning opportunities that each obstacle presents and use them to grow and adapt.

- **Trust the Process:** Bootstrapping is not for the faint of heart, but if you're willing to put in the time and effort, it can lead to long-term success. Believe in your vision, abilities, and the worth of your product or service. Believe that your hard work and dedication will be rewarded in the end.

You'll be better prepared to navigate the inevitable ups and downs of bootstrapping if you cultivate patience. Remember that rapid growth is not always indicative of success and that a slower, more sustainable path can lead to a stronger, more resilient business in the long run.

Cultivating a Growth Mindset

For bootstrapped entrepreneurs, a growth mindset is essential because it allows them to embrace challenges, learn from setbacks, and adapt to changing circumstances. Adopting a growth mindset allows you to foster a culture of continuous improvement and innovation, which is critical for your bootstrapped startup's long-term success.

- **Stay Curious:** Develop a sense of wonder and a thirst for knowledge. Seek out new information, ideas, and perspectives on a regular basis to help inform your decisions and drive innovation. You can identify new opportunities and stay ahead of the curve in a rapidly changing business landscape by remaining open to learning.

- **Encourage Adaptability:** Adaptability is essential in the fast-paced world of startups. You can pivot and adjust your strategies in response to market changes, customer feedback, and other external factors if you have a growth mindset. Accept change and be willing to shift gears when necessary, as flexibility can provide a significant competitive advantage.

- **Encourage Continuous Improvement:** Establish a culture of continuous improvement within your startup in which every team member is encouraged to learn, grow, and contribute to the company's success. Make opportunities for skill development and professional growth available, and evaluate

your progress and performance on a regular basis
to identify areas for improvement.

- **Set Stretch Goals:** Encourage your team to set lofty
  goals that push them outside of their comfort
  zones. Stretch goals can spark creativity, increase
  motivation, and propel exceptional performance.
  You can unlock the full potential of your
  bootstrapped startup by striving for the
  extraordinary.

Bootstrapped entrepreneurs who cultivate a growth
mindset can navigate the complexities of starting a business
from scratch, learn from their mistakes, and continuously
adapt and improve. This mindset is essential not only for
individual success, but also for establishing a thriving, innovative, and resilient startup capable of overcoming the challenges of the entrepreneurial journey.

Balancing Passion and Rationality

Finding the right balance between the passion that drives
your startup idea and the rationality needed to make sound
business decisions and implement effective growth strategies
is critical. While passion can drive innovation and motivate
you to overcome obstacles, it is critical to combine it with a
practical mindset to ensure the long-term success of your
startup.

- **Be Receptive to Feedback:** Accept feedback from
  your customers, advisors, and mentors.
  Constructive criticism can help you improve your
  product or service, identify potential pitfalls, and
  make more informed business decisions. While it is

important to believe in your concept, don't let your enthusiasm blind you to valuable insights from others.

- **Test and iterate:** Because resources are limited as a bootstrapped entrepreneur, it is critical to validate your idea before investing significant time and money. Adopt a lean approach by developing and testing a minimum viable product (MVP). Use the feedback you receive to iterate and improve your offering, ensuring that it meets the needs and expectations of your customers.

- **Create a Viable Business Model:** While passion can inspire you to create innovative products or services, it is critical to develop a viable business model to support the growth of your startup. Consider revenue streams, pricing strategies, and customer acquisition costs to ensure your company's financial viability over time.

- **Maintain Your Long-Term Vision:** While it is critical to focus on immediate tasks and goals, don't lose sight of your long-term vision. Create a growth roadmap for your startup and reassess your strategies on a regular basis to ensure they are in line with your overall goals. You'll be better equipped to navigate the challenges and opportunities that lie ahead if you balance your passion with a rational approach.

You'll be well-positioned to make informed decisions, implement effective growth strategies, and ensure the success of your bootstrapped startup if you strike the right balance of passion and rationality. Remember that the combination of enthusiasm and practicality is a powerful force that can propel your startup to new heights as you continue on your entrepreneurial journey.

With these insights in hand, you're ready to move on to Chapter 3: Validating Your Idea on a Budget, where you'll learn invaluable strategies for testing and refining your startup idea without breaking the bank.

3

VALIDATING YOUR IDEA ON A BUDGET

∾

As I made 150 calls per day, connecting with potential clients in the trades and construction industries, the sound of the phone ringing became all too familiar. Over time, I began to notice a pattern: a significant portion of these clients were having difficulty generating leads and revenue. This recurring issue piqued my interest and, in the end, validated my idea for my first business, which aimed to alleviate this pain point for clients in this niche market.

Fast forward to my current endeavor, Better Boss Brands, where I've seen firsthand the difficulties that businesses face when attempting to implement a streamlined sales system. As a founder, I've felt the frustration of poorly optimized sales process and software, and I've witnessed the same issues for our clients. This encounter has motivated me to find a solution to this widespread issue.

These personal anecdotes highlight the significance of validating your idea before committing fully to it. In this chapter, we'll look at how to validate your startup idea on a budget, as well as strategies for ensuring that you're addressing a genuine market need.

Remember that the foundation of a successful bootstrapped startup is solving a genuine problem, so take the time to validate your idea and put your company on the right track.

The Importance of Idea Validation

As we proceed through Chapter 3, it is critical to comprehend the significance of idea validation in the world of bootstrapped startups. Validating your idea before investing significant time and resources is an important step in the entrepreneurial process. It allows you to test the waters and ensure that your venture has a reasonable chance of success, ultimately saving you from investing in a project that is not viable.

The Value of Idea Validation:

- **Risk Reduction**: As a bootstrapped entrepreneur, you have limited resources. Validating your idea reduces the risk of committing too much time and money to a project that may not have a high market demand. You can avoid costly mistakes and make more informed decisions if you identify potential flaws and weaknesses early on.

- **Market Demand:** Validating your idea ensures that there is a genuine market need for your product or service. Understanding the specific pain points and challenges that your target audience faces allows you to create a solution that effectively addresses those needs while also appealing to your potential customers.

- **Improved Resource Allocation:** Validating your idea gives you a better understanding of your target market and their preferences. This knowledge allows you to better allocate your limited resources, focusing on areas that will have the greatest impact.

- Validation *assists you in identifying the essential features and functions of your product or service*, allowing you to prioritize and streamline development. You can reduce development time and cost while still delivering a product that meets your customers' needs by focusing on the core components.

- **Confidence:** Validating your idea gives you more confidence in your startup venture. You'll be more motivated to pursue your goals and more likely to attract the attention of potential partners, investors, and customers if you have evidence that your product or service addresses a genuine market need.

- **Improved Adaptability:** Idea validation is a continuous process that requires feedback and adjustment. By adopting this iterative approach, you will become more adaptable and better prepared to respond to market changes, ensuring your startup's relevance and competitiveness.

Finally, idea validation is critical to the success of bootstrapped startups. It assists you in confirming your venture's viability, optimizing resource allocation, and improving your product or service based on feedback from your target market. You will be better equipped to navigate the challenges of entrepreneurship and increase your chances of success if you take the time to validate your idea.

Defining Your Target Market

We will now look at how to define your target market. Understanding your target market is critical for the success of your bootstrapped startup because it allows you to tailor your product or service to their specific needs, preferences, and pain points.

Identifying Your Market:

- **Determine Your Ideal Customer:** Begin by developing a thorough profile of your ideal customer. Consider age, gender, income, location, and occupation, as well as psychographic factors such as interests, values, and lifestyle. Understanding your ideal customer's characteristics allows you to more effectively target your marketing efforts and create a product or service that truly resonates with them.

- *Conduct thorough market research to gain insights* into the behavior, preferences, and needs of your target audience. Data can be gathered from a variety of sources, including industry reports, surveys, social media, and online forums. This data will assist you in making more informed decisions about your product or service offering, pricing, and marketing strategies.

- **Analyze Your Competitors' Offerings:** Understanding your competitors' offerings is critical for defining your target market. Analyze your competitors' strengths and weaknesses, and identify any gaps or opportunities in the market that you can exploit. You can appeal to a specific segment of the market that may be underserved or overlooked by differentiating yourself from the competition.

- Validate your assumptions about your target market *by directly engaging with potential customers*. Use surveys, interviews, or focus groups to gather feedback on your product or service concept. This direct interaction will assist you in refining your offering and ensuring that it meets the genuine needs and preferences of your target audience.

- **Refine Your Market Segmentation:** Refine your market segmentation based on the insights gleaned from your research and customer feedback. This could mean narrowing your target audience to a more specific niche or broadening it to include a broader range of potential customers. You can ensure that your product or service remains relevant and appealing by constantly refining your target market.

- **Monitor and Adjust:** Determining your target market is a continuous process that necessitates constant monitoring and adjustment. Maintain a keen awareness of changes in market conditions, customer preferences, and the competitive landscape. To keep your startup relevant and competitive, reevaluate and update your target market definition on a regular basis.

Defining your target market is an important step in the journey of a bootstrapped startup. Understanding your target audience's needs, preferences, and pain points will allow you to create a product or service that meets their needs while also standing out in the marketplace. This focused approach will ultimately improve your chances of success and allow you to make the most of your limited resources.

Pre-Sales and Crowdfunding

Let's look at how pre-sales and crowdfunding campaigns can be used as powerful validation methods for your bootstrapped startup.

Crowdfunding and Pre-Sales:

- Pre-sales and crowdfunding campaigns *provide unique opportunities to validate your startup idea,* assess market demand, and generate early revenue, all while reducing the financial risk of launching a new product or service.

- Pre-sales are when *you sell your product or service before it is fully developed or available.* This method allows you to gauge interest in your offering and generate early revenue to help fund its development. To successfully launch a pre-sale campaign, you must develop a compelling offer and promotional strategy that resonates with your target market and generates excitement about your upcoming launch.

- Crowdfunding platforms such as Kickstarter and Indiegogo *enable entrepreneurs to raise funds for their projects by offering rewards or equity* in exchange for monetary contributions from backers. These campaigns can be used to validate your product or service by demonstrating market demand and creating buzz around it. Strong storytelling, engaging promotional materials, and a clear value proposition that appeals to potential backers are frequently used in successful crowdfunding campaigns.

The Benefits of Pre-Sales and Crowdfunding:

- **Market Validation:** Pre-sales and crowdfunding campaigns both provide direct feedback from your target market, allowing you to assess demand for your product or service and fine-tune your offering based on real-world feedback.

- **Early Revenue:** These methods can generate critical early revenue to aid in the development and launch of your product or service, reducing the financial strain on your bootstrapped startup.

- **Marketing and Exposure:** Before your official launch, pre-sales and crowdfunding campaigns can generate buzz about your product or service, providing valuable exposure and assisting in the development of a loyal customer base.

- Pre-sales and crowdfunding campaigns can *reduce the overall risk of launching a new product or service* by securing early revenue and validating market demand.

To reap the most benefits from pre-sales and crowdfunding, carefully plan your campaign, engage your target audience, and deliver a compelling value proposition. You will not only be validating your idea, but you will also be building momentum for your bootstrapped startup and laying the groundwork for long-term success.

Minimum Viable Product (MVP)

Continuing with Chapter 3, consider the concept of a Minimum Viable Product (MVP) and its role in idea validation, especially for bootstrapped startups with limited resources.

MVP (Minimum Viable Product):

An MVP is a condensed version of your product or service that only includes the essential features. An MVP's primary goal is to test the viability of your idea, gather feedback from early users, and iterate on the product based on the insights gained. This method allows you to validate your startup idea and make informed decisions about its development without committing significant time and resources to a full-fledged launch.

Making an MVP on a Tight Budget:

- **Prioritize Core Features:** Identify the essential features that address the pain points of your target market and provide a solution to their problem. To keep development costs and complexity to a minimum, include only these core features in your MVP.

- **Use Existing Tools and Platforms:** Make use of existing tools, platforms, and frameworks to build your MVP quickly and affordably. This may entail creating a functional prototype of your product or service using website builders, app development platforms, or open-source software.

- **Choose Low-Cost Development Methods:** To build your MVP on a tight budget, consider hiring freelance developers, collaborating with technical co-founders, or utilizing no-code/low-code development tools.

- Once your MVP is complete, *share it with a small group of potential users, customers, or stakeholders* to gather valuable feedback. Use this feedback to improve your product and address any issues or concerns that arise during the testing phase.

- **Iterate and Improve:** Make necessary changes to your product or service based on feedback, and continue testing and refining until you're confident that your offering meets the needs of your target market.

You can quickly and cost-effectively validate your startup idea and make data-driven decisions about its future development by creating an MVP on a limited budget. This strategy allows you to reduce risk while increasing your chances of success, ensuring that your bootstrapped startup is well-positioned to thrive in a competitive market landscape.

Seeking Feedback from Mentors and Industry Experts

Moving on, let's talk about the importance of seeking feedback from experienced mentors and industry experts, as well as how to approach them and incorporate their insights into your validation process.

Seeking Mentors and Industry Experts for Feedback:

Mentors and industry experts can provide invaluable insights and experience to entrepreneurs attempting to validate their startup idea. These individuals can offer a unique perspective on your product or service, assist you in identifying potential pitfalls, and advise you on how to overcome challenges that may arise during the validation process.

Getting in touch with mentors and industry experts:

- **Identify Relevant People:** Look for mentors and experts with experience in your industry or a thorough understanding of the problem you're attempting to solve. Successful entrepreneurs, investors, academics, and professionals with relevant expertise may be included.

- **Be Respectful and Professional:** Always be respectful and professional when contacting potential mentors or industry experts. Explain your startup concept, the stage you're in, and the specific feedback or guidance you're looking for.

- **Take Advantage of Networking Events and Online Platforms:** Attend industry events, conferences, or workshops to meet potential mentors or experts. Alternatively, to make connections and seek advice, use online platforms such as LinkedIn or industry-specific forums.

Recognize that mentors and industry experts are frequently busy and may receive numerous requests for assistance. Provide value in exchange for their time and insights, whether by sharing your own expertise, providing a service, or otherwise supporting their endeavors.

Including Feedback in the Validation Process:

- **Be Open to Criticism:** Accept constructive criticism and be willing to modify your startup idea in response to it. Recognize that this process has the potential to strengthen your offering and boost its chances of success.

- **Prioritize Feedback:** Not all feedback will be equally useful or relevant to your startup idea. Consider the source of each piece of feedback and prioritize the most relevant and helpful insights.

- **Implement Changes:** Respond to feedback by making necessary changes to your product, service, or strategy. Prepare to iterate and refine your offering in response to feedback from mentors and industry experts.

- **Maintain an Ongoing Relationship:** Stay in touch with the mentors and experts who provide valuable feedback, informing them of your progress and seeking their advice when new challenges arise.

By soliciting feedback from mentors and industry experts, you can more effectively validate your startup idea, identify potential issues, and ensure that your bootstrapped venture is well-prepared to succeed in the market.

Iterating and Pivoting Based on Validation Results

As we wrap up this chapter, consider how important it is to be open to iteration and pivot your idea based on validation findings. We'll also recommend ways to improve your product or service offering to better meet market needs and demands.

Based on the Validation Results, iterate and pivot:

- During the validation process, *you may come across unexpected findings, feedback, or changing market conditions*. It is critical for the long-term success of your bootstrapped startup to be open to iteration and pivoting your idea in response to these new insights.

- **Maintain Flexibility and Adaptability:** Accept that your initial idea may not be perfect and that it will most likely evolve over time. Prepare to make changes and revisions based on the feedback and validation results.

- **Analyze Validation Data:** Thoroughly review the data you collected during the validation process, looking for trends, patterns, and insights that can help you decide what to do next. Look for areas where your product or service could be improved or where you could better serve your target market.

- **Accept Experimentation:** Consider your validation process to be a continuous series of experiments, each designed to test specific assumptions about your product or service. Be willing to experiment with new approaches and strategies to address the challenges and opportunities that you discover.

- If your validation results indicate that your initial idea is not viable or *that there is a more promising opportunity to pursue, be prepared to pivot your startup in a new direction*. This could entail changing your product or service offering, focusing on a different market segment, or implementing a new business model.

You will be better equipped to refine your product or service offering and ensure that it meets the needs and demands of your target market if you remain open to iteration and pivoting based on validation results. This adaptability will be important as a bootstrapped entrepreneur to maximize your chances of success.

After you've validated and refined your startup idea, it's time to move on to the next stage of your entrepreneurial journey: creating a lean business plan. In the following chapter, we'll look at how to develop an effective and agile business plan to support the growth and success of your bootstrapped venture.

4

CRAFTING A LEAN BUSINESS PLAN

⁓

I didn't have a clear business plan in place when I started my first company. This resulted in unnecessary expenditures and a constant change of direction. I didn't know what I didn't know at the time, and I had to learn by doing while juggling my limited time and resources.

Fast forward to today, and I've created a comprehensive business plan for Better Boss Brands that outlines our ideal brand persona, their problems, and how my skills can solve them. In all areas of the business, I've set SMART goals for one month, quarterly, yearly, and even five years. Furthermore, I have a clear vision of how to create multiple income streams in one industry by leveraging my experience, understanding, and dependability.

By the end of this chapter, you'll have a solid understanding of the components of a lean business plan and how to create one that will put your bootstrapped startup on the right track.

The Importance of a Lean Business Plan

A lean business plan functions as both a growth strategy and a tool for attracting potential investors. It's a streamlined version of a traditional business plan that focuses on the most important aspects of your startup and is designed to be adaptable to the ever-changing entrepreneurial environment.

Let's go over the importance of a lean business plan for bootstrapped startups in greater detail.

- A lean business plan *provides a clear outline of your startup's objectives, strategies, and tactics, guiding your decision-making process and keeping your team focused* on the most important tasks. It enables you to effectively prioritize and allocate resources, ensuring that every decision is consistent with your long-term vision and goals.

- **Attracting potential investors:** Although bootstrapped startups rely primarily on the resources of their founders, you may need to seek external funding at some point. A well-crafted lean business plan shows that you have a clear vision, understand your market, and have devised a viable growth strategy. When pitching your startup to potential investors, this can be a valuable asset.

- **Encourage accountability:** With a lean business plan in place, you and your team members will have a common understanding of the startup's direction and goals. This creates a sense of accountability, which motivates everyone to stay on track and work toward the same goals.

- **Allowing for adaptability:** A lean business plan is designed to be adaptable, allowing you to respond quickly to new opportunities or challenges. You can ensure that your strategies and tactics remain relevant and effective in the face of a constantly changing business landscape by reviewing and updating your plan on a regular basis.

- **Saving time and resources:** A lean business plan focuses on the most important aspects of your startup, removing any unnecessary elements that would otherwise take up valuable time and resources. This simplified approach allows you to focus your efforts on what is truly important, increasing your chances of success.

In conclusion, a lean business plan is essential for bootstrapped startups because it serves as a growth roadmap, a tool for attracting potential investors, and a way to foster accountability and adaptability within your team. You can increase the likelihood of your startup's success and better navigate the challenges that come with building a business from the ground up by creating a lean business plan.

Identifying Your Value Proposition

A value proposition is a concise statement that explains how your bootstrapped startup's product or service addresses the needs and pain points of your target market. A strong value proposition is critical for distinguishing your startup from competitors and persuading potential customers to select your offering over others.

Here are some pointers for developing and communicating a strong value proposition for your bootstrapped startup:

- **Understand your target market:** Begin by gaining a thorough understanding of your target market's needs, preferences, and pain points. Investigate your market thoroughly and speak with potential customers to identify the specific problems they are experiencing and how your product or service can help them.

- **Focus on the benefits:** Rather than focusing on the features of your product or service, your value proposition should emphasize the benefits it provides. Consider the benefits that your offering can provide to your customers, such as saving time, increasing efficiency, or improving their quality of life.

- **Determine your distinct selling points (USPs):** Consider what distinguishes your product or service from the competition. Superior quality, innovative technology, exceptional customer service, or a lower price could be your USPs. Make sure to emphasize these distinguishing features in your value proposition.

- **Be concise and clear:** Your value proposition should be a concise, clear statement that communicates your offering's core benefits and USPs. Avoid jargon and buzzwords, and instead strive for simplicity and clarity in your language.

- **Test and refine your value proposition:** Once you've developed your initial value proposition, put it to the test with your target market to get feedback and make any necessary changes. This iterative process will assist in ensuring that your value proposition resonates with potential customers and accurately reflects the unique value of your product or service.

A well-defined value proposition can be an effective tool for attracting customers and distinguishing your bootstrapped startup in the market. You can create a compelling message that resonates with your target market and drives growth for your startup by focusing on the benefits and unique selling points of your product or service and ensuring that your value proposition is clear and concise.

Market Analysis and Target Customer

Understanding your market and identifying your target customers are critical steps in launching a profitable bootstrapped startup. Conducting a thorough market analysis and gaining insights into the needs, preferences, and pain points of your target customers will allow you to tailor your product or service offering, marketing strategy, and overall business approach.

Here are some important steps to take when conducting market research and identifying target customers:

- **Overview of the industry:** Begin by gathering information about the industry in general. Investigate market size, growth trends, key players, and any potential entry barriers. This will help you understand the market landscape and identify opportunities and challenges that your startup may face.

- *Analyze your direct and indirect competitors* to learn about their strengths, weaknesses, and market positioning. This will assist you in identifying market gaps that your startup can fill as well as differentiating your product or service from existing offerings.

- **Customer segmentation:** Divide your target market into distinct segments based on demographics, geography, behavioral patterns, and psychographics. This will allow you to better understand each segment's specific needs and preferences and tailor your offering accordingly.

- **Customer needs and pain points:** Conduct primary research, such as interviews, surveys, and focus groups, to gain insights into the needs, preferences, and pain points of your target customers. This will assist you in identifying the specific problems that your product or service can solve and in developing a compelling value proposition.

- **Market trends and opportunities:** Monitor emerging trends and changes in your industry, as well as broader market shifts that may affect your target customers. This will assist you in staying ahead of the competition and identifying new opportunities for growth and innovation.

- **SWOT analysis:** To assess your startup's market position, conduct a SWOT (Strengths, Weaknesses, Opportunities, Threats) analysis. This will assist you in identifying your competitive advantages and areas for improvement, as well as potential market opportunities and challenges.

You can develop a tailored product or service offering,

marketing strategy, and overall business approach that addresses their needs, preferences, and pain points by conducting a thorough market analysis and gaining a deep understanding of your target customers. This will not only increase your chances of success, but will also help you stand out in your industry's competitive landscape.

Defining Your Business Model

Creating a viable business model is an essential first step for any bootstrapped startup. A well-defined business model assists you in determining how your startup will create, deliver, and capture market value. Consider revenue streams, pricing strategies, and customer acquisition channels when developing your business model.

Here's an overview of these key components, as well as some advice on how to create a viable business model:

- *Identify the various revenue streams that your startup can generate*. Direct sales, subscriptions, advertising, licensing, and even affiliate marketing are all possibilities. Consider diversifying your revenue streams to reduce risk and increase cash flow stability.

- **Pricing strategies:** Choose a pricing strategy that is appropriate for your target market and competitive landscape. Pricing models such as cost-plus pricing, value-based pricing, competitive pricing, and tiered pricing are available. It is critical to strike a balance between covering your costs, maximizing profitability, and remaining market competitive.

- **Channels of customer acquisition:** Determine the most efficient and cost-effective channels for reaching and acquiring your target customers. Focus on channels that provide the best return on investment (ROI) with the least amount of money up front for bootstrapped startups. Organic search, social media marketing, content marketing, email marketing, and referral programs are some examples.

- **Value delivery:** Describe how your startup intends to provide its product or service to customers. The entire customer journey, from discovery to purchase and beyond, is covered. Consider user experience, customer service, and any after-sales services that may be required to ensure customer satisfaction and loyalty.

- Identify the *key partnerships and resources you'll need to successfully execute* your business model. This may include suppliers, manufacturers, distributors, or even strategic partners who can assist you in entering new markets or gaining new customers.

- **Cost structure:** Examine the costs associated with your business model, such as fixed and variable costs, as well as any required upfront investments. This will assist you in comprehending the financial viability of your business model and informing your pricing strategy.

By taking these factors into account when developing your business model, you can create a strategy that aligns with your startup's goals and resources while also addressing the needs of your target market. As your startup grows and the market evolves, remember to constantly assess and refine your business model to ensure it remains viable and competitive over time.

Establishing SMART Goals and Objectives

Setting specific, measurable, achievable, relevant, and time-bound (SMART) goals and objectives is critical for guiding the growth and development of your startup. SMART goals give your team a clear direction, help prioritize tasks and resources, and allow you to track progress and success.

Here's a rundown of the SMART criteria and why each one is critical for your startup:

- **Specific:** Define your goals and objectives clearly so that everyone on your team understands what needs to be done. A specific goal should answer questions such as what you want to accomplish, why it is important, and how you intend to accomplish it. Ambiguous goals can cause confusion and make tracking progress difficult.

- **Measurable:** Create quantifiable indicators to help you track your progress and determine whether or not the goal has been met. Metrics such as revenue, user growth, or customer satisfaction scores are examples of measurable goals. Monitoring these metrics on a regular basis allows you to make data-driven decisions and adjust your strategies as needed.

- **Achievable:** Set challenging but realistic goals that take into account your startup's resources, capabilities, and market conditions. Overly ambitious goals can demoralize your team and lead to burnout, whereas easily attainable goals may not fully realize the potential of your startup. Strive for a happy medium that promotes growth and keeps your team motivated.

- **Relevant:** Make sure your goals and objectives are in line with the overall mission, vision, and strategic priorities of your startup. Relevant goals keep you focused on what is most important to your business, avoiding distractions and wasting valuable resources on unrelated pursuits.

- **Time-bound:** Set deadlines for your goals and objectives to instill urgency and hold your team accountable. Time-bound goals also assist you in more effectively prioritizing tasks and allocating resources, ensuring you stay on track to achieve your desired outcomes.

Involve your team in the process of developing SMART goals and objectives for your startup to ensure buy-in and commitment. As your startup grows, review and adjust your goals on a regular basis, and use them to inform your decision-making, resource allocation, and performance evaluations. You can keep your bootstrapped startup focused and on track for long-term success by setting SMART goals.

Outlining a Marketing and Sales Strategy

Developing a marketing and sales strategy is critical for promoting your bootstrapped startup's products or services to your target audience, especially if you have a limited budget.

Here are some ideas to help you develop a low-cost marketing and sales strategy for your startup:

- **Define your target market:** Determine your ideal customers' needs, preferences, and pain points. This will assist you in crafting a tailored marketing message and concentrating your efforts on the channels and platforms most likely to reach them.

- **Utilize low-cost marketing channels:** To reach your target audience, use low-cost marketing channels such as social media, email marketing, content marketing, and search engine optimization (SEO). These channels can assist you in increasing brand awareness, engaging potential customers, and driving website traffic without incurring significant costs.

- *Create a strong online presence* by creating a professional website and remaining active on relevant social media platforms. A strong online presence will aid in the establishment of credibility, engagement with your target audience, and lead generation.

- Make use of content marketing by *creating valuable and informative content that appeals to your target audience*. Share blog posts, articles, videos, and infographics to demonstrate your expertise and establish your startup as an industry thought leader.

- Attend industry events, participate in online forums, and *collaborate with other entrepreneurs and influencers in your niche*. Without spending a lot of money, networking and partnerships can help you generate buzz and reach new customer segments.

- **Create a referral program:** Encourage happy customers to tell their friends and colleagues about your startup. Word-of-mouth marketing is not only inexpensive, but it also aids in the development of trust and credibility for your brand.

- **Monitor and analyze performance:** Monitor and analyze the performance of your marketing and sales efforts on a regular basis. To measure your success and adjust your strategy, use tools like Google Analytics and social media analytics.

- **Optimize your sales process:** Use customer relationship management (CRM) tools and sales automation to streamline your sales process. This can help you manage leads more effectively, track customer interactions, and close deals more efficiently.

You can create a marketing and sales plan that effectively promotes your bootstrapped startup's products or services to your target audience while minimizing costs by implementing these strategies. To ensure continued growth and success, review and adjust your strategy on a regular basis based on performance data and market trends.

Operational Planning and Process Optimization

Creating an efficient operational plan is critical for bootstrapped startups to optimize processes, effectively allocate resources, and reduce costs.

When developing an operational plan for your bootstrapped startup, consider the following key elements:

- **Process improvement:** Evaluate your current processes and identify areas for improvement. To increase efficiency and reduce time spent on manual tasks, streamline workflows, eliminate redundant tasks, and implement automation tools where possible.

- Allocate resources strategically in order to maximize their impact on your business objectives. P*rioritize investments in areas with the greatest growth potential and return on investment (ROI).* Based on performance data and market trends, continuously assess and adjust your resource allocation.

- Cost-cutting measures include *identifying and reducing unnecessary expenses* such as office space, subscriptions, and equipment. Adopt a frugal mindset and look for low-cost alternatives, such as open-source software, remote work, or outsourcing non-core tasks to freelancers or specialized service providers.

- **Management of suppliers and vendors:** Build strong relationships with your suppliers and vendors. To reduce costs and improve cash flow, negotiate favorable terms such as bulk discounts, extended payment terms, or better shipping rates.

- Quality control measures should be implemented to *ensure that your product or service consistently meets customer expectations*. This can help you reduce returns, refunds, and customer complaints while also building a strong brand reputation.

- Risk management entails *identifying potential risks and challenges that may affect the operations* of your startup, such as supply chain disruptions, regulatory changes, or natural disasters. Create backup plans to mitigate these risks and ensure business continuity.

- Establish key performance indicators (KPIs) *to monitor the efficiency and effectiveness of your operational processes*. Review and analyze performance data on a regular basis to identify areas for improvement and adjust your operational plan accordingly.

You can create an efficient operational plan that supports the growth and sustainability of your bootstrapped startup by focusing on process optimization, resource allocation, and cost reduction. To ensure continued success, review and update your operational plan on a regular basis based on performance data, market trends, and changes in your business environment.

Building a Strong Team

Putting together a talented, motivated, and cohesive team is critical to the success of your bootstrapped startup. A strong team can drive innovation, boost productivity, and assist your company in overcoming obstacles.

Here are some pointers to help you attract and retain top talent for your startup:

- **Define your company culture and values:** A well-defined company culture and set of values can assist you in attracting like-minded individuals who share your vision and are committed to the success of your startup. To ensure a good cultural fit, clearly communicate your mission, values, and expectations during the recruitment process.

- While bootstrapped startups may have limited resources, *offering competitive compensation packages is important for attracting and retaining top talent*. To make your startup more appealing to potential employees, consider offering equity, performance-based bonuses, or other non-monetary perks.

- **Provide opportunities for growth and development:** Top talent is often drawn to startups that provide opportunities for growth and development. Encourage continuous learning and give your team members access to training, workshops, and mentorship programs to help them learn new skills and advance in their careers.

- **Create a work environment that is flexible and supportive:** Create a work environment that promotes flexibility, work-life balance, and open communication. Encourage remote work, flexible schedules, and team collaboration to foster a positive environment that fosters creativity and productivity.

- **Recognize and reward accomplishments:** Recognize and reward your team members on a regular basis for their hard work and accomplishments. This can improve morale, increase job satisfaction, and foster loyalty to your startup.

- *Create a diverse and inclusive team* by emphasizing the importance of diversity and inclusion during the hiring process. A diverse and inclusive team brings distinct perspectives, experiences, and skills to the table, which can spur innovation and improve decision-making.

- **Encourage team bonding and collaboration:** Plan team-building activities and events to help your team members bond and trust one another. Encourage open communication and collaboration, as this can lead to more creative problem-solving and solutions.

- **Communicate your vision and goals:** Share your startup's vision and goals with your team members on a regular basis to ensure they understand how their work fits into the bigger picture. In the long run, this can help keep them motivated and engaged.

By concentrating on these strategies, you can create a strong team dedicated to the success of your bootstrapped startup. Keep in mind that attracting and retaining top talent is an ongoing process, so evaluate and adjust your recruitment and retention strategies as needed.

Financial Projections and Budgeting

It is vital for the success of your bootstrapped startup to create realistic financial projections and budgets. Financial planning that is accurate allows you to make informed decisions, allocate resources efficiently, and track your progress.

Here's a high-level overview of the process, with an emphasis on the importance of conservative estimates and regular financial reviews:

- Begin by *estimating the initial costs of your startup*, including equipment, inventory, and initial marketing expenses. Take into account any ongoing expenses, such as rent, salaries, and utilities. To avoid overestimating your financial capabilities, make conservative estimates.

- *Project the revenue of your startup* based on your target market size, pricing strategy, and sales projections. Estimates should be realistic and conservative, as overly optimistic projections can lead to poor decision-making and financial strain.

- *Create a cash flow projection* that details your startup's incoming and outgoing funds over a specific time period. This will assist you in identifying potential cash flow gaps and ensuring you have sufficient funds to cover your expenses.

- *Create a profit and loss statement* that summarizes the revenue, costs, and expenses of your startup. This document will assist you in determining the profitability of your startup and identifying areas for cost reduction and revenue optimization.

- *Create a budget* that details your startup's financial plan, including projected revenue, expenses, and cash flow. To ensure your startup's financial stability, set aside funds for unexpected expenses and contingencies.

- *Set financial goals that are in line with the overall goals* of your startup. These objectives will assist you in measuring your progress and staying on track to achieve your desired results.

- Review and *update your financial projections and budgets on a regular basis* to account for changes in your startup's environment or performance. This will assist you in maintaining a realistic view of your financial situation and making informed decisions in the future.

- Monitor the *financial performance of your startup in relation to your projections and budget.* This will assist you in identifying areas where you are exceeding expectations and areas where you need to improve.

You can create realistic financial projections and budgets for your bootstrapped startup by following these steps. Remember that conservative estimates and regular financial reviews are critical to your startup's financial health and long-term success.

Regularly Reviewing and Updating Your Lean Business Plan

A lean business plan is not meant to be a static document. Instead, think of it as a living document that evolves alongside your startup. Regularly reviewing and updating your plan is critical to ensuring that it remains relevant and effectively guides your business.

Here are pointers for keeping your lean business plan current:

- *Make time to review your business plan on a regular basis* (e.g., quarterly or biannually). This will help you stay focused on your objectives and ensure that your plan is still relevant to your current priorities and market conditions.

- *Evaluate your startup's progress toward its goals* and objectives. Determine where you have met or exceeded expectations, as well as where you have fallen short. This will allow you to make necessary adjustments and more effectively allocate resources.

- *Stay up to date on developments in your industry* and target market, such as emerging trends, competitors, and customer preferences. To ensure your startup's success, update your market analysis and competitive landscape sections to reflect these changes.

- Your goals and objectives may change as your startup grows and evolves. *Prepare to revise your SMART goals* and objectives to reflect your current priorities and long-term vision.

- As previously stated, it is essential to review and update your financial projections and budgets on a regular basis. *Maintain a realistic financial plan* that accounts for any changes in your startup's performance or market conditions.

- *Your marketing and sales strategy may need to be adjusted* as your startup grows or as you learn more about the preferences and habits of your

target audience. Make any necessary changes to
ensure your strategy remains effective and drives
growth.

- As your startup grows, ***you may need to reevaluate
  your team composition and organizational
  structure***. Ensure that your team is still well-suited
  to meet the current and future needs of your
  startup.

- ***Keep your team, investors, and other stakeholders
  up to date*** on any changes to your business plan.
  This will help to ensure that everyone is on the
  same page and understands your company's
  current priorities and direction.

By treating your lean business plan as a living document
that is regularly updated, you will ensure that it continues to
serve as a valuable roadmap for the growth and success of
your startup.

Now that we've covered how to write a lean business
plan, we can move on to Chapter 5: Budgeting and Financial
Management, where we'll go over how to effectively manage
your startup's finances.

5

BUDGETING AND FINANCIAL MANAGEMENT

~

When I first started bootstrapping my own business, I was under a lot of financial stress, both personally and professionally. I made significant sacrifices during that time, and the weight of financial responsibilities weighed heavily on me.

Before generating any revenue, I obtained a $15,000 line of credit from Chase and had to rely on it to get my business off the ground. To effectively manage my finances, I set up my financial records in QuickBooks, which allowed me to see reports, cut costs, track expenses, and keep an eye on our finances.

Over time, I began to concentrate on acquiring clients with recurring revenue, with monthly fees ranging from $3,000 to $10,000. By automatically charging these clients on the first of each month, I was able to better forecast our financial situation and alleviate the stress of starting from scratch each month.

Let's now look at the various aspects of budgeting and financial management for bootstrapped businesses.

Importance of Budgeting

Budgeting is an important part of financial management for any business, but it is especially important for bootstrapped startups. As a bootstrapped entrepreneur, you have limited resources and funds, so you must allocate your resources effectively and responsibly. Budgeting has a direct impact on your company's overall financial health and growth.

Budgeting is important for several reasons, including:

- **Resource allocation:** A well-defined budget allows you to efficiently prioritize and allocate your resources. By identifying the most critical areas of your business that require funding, you can concentrate your efforts on activities that directly contribute to the growth and success of your startup.

- *Budgeting allows you to keep track of your expenses* and manage them effectively. This prevents you from overspending on non-essential purchases, allowing you to maintain a healthy financial position and avoid potential financial crises.

- **Setting financial goals:** A budget allows you to set realistic financial goals for your startup, giving you a clear roadmap for growth. Setting specific goals allows you to track your progress and make adjustments as needed to stay on track.

- Budgeting allows you to *identify potential risks and uncertainties in your company's financial landscape.* You can mitigate potential negative effects on your business by proactively addressing these risks and developing contingency plans.

- **Making informed business decisions:** A budget provides you with the data and insights you need to make informed business decisions. Understanding your financial position allows you to better evaluate potential opportunities and make decisions that align with the goals and objectives of your startup.

- **Attracting investors:** Although bootstrapped startups typically rely on their own resources, external funding may be required at some point. A well-prepared budget shows potential investors that you have a firm grasp on your finances.

- Finally, budgeting is an important part of a bootstrapped startup's financial management strategy. *A well-crafted budget not only allows you to effectively allocate resources and manage costs,* but it also allows you to set realistic financial goals, mitigate risks, make informed decisions, and attract potential investors when necessary.

Recognizing the importance of budgeting and devoting time and effort to creating and maintaining a comprehensive budget can significantly improve the financial health, stability, and chances of success of your startup in the long run. Your bootstrapped startup will be better prepared to face challenges and seize opportunities if it has a solid budgeting foundation.

Creating a Realistic Budget

When creating a comprehensive and realistic budget for your bootstrapped startup, it's critical to take into account a variety of factors that can affect your financial health.

Here are some important steps to take in order to create a budget that accurately reflects your startup's financial needs and goals:

- *Estimate your expected revenues* based on market research, historical sales data, and industry benchmarks. Keep your projections conservative to avoid overestimating your income, which could lead to overspending.

- *Identify and list all fixed expenses*, such as rent, insurance, salaries, and utilities. These are costs that remain relatively constant regardless of revenue levels and should be budgeted for.

- **Variable Expenses:** Determine your variable expenses, which vary depending on the level of activity in your business. Marketing expenses, production costs, and shipping fees are some examples. Consider the relationship between your revenue and the associated expenses as you estimate these costs.

- *Plan for unexpected events and emergencies* by allocating a portion of your budget to this purpose. This could be a cash reserve or a contingency fund. Having a financial safety net can help you navigate unexpected challenges without jeopardizing the stability of your business.

- **Profit Margins:** Subtract your total expenses from your total revenues to calculate your projected profit margins. This will give you an idea of your company's financial viability and help you identify areas where you can improve profitability.

- **Regular Budget Reviews:** Conduct regular budget reviews to track your progress and make necessary adjustments. This will assist you in staying on track with your financial objectives and identifying any gaps between your projections and actual performance.

- *Allow for some budget flexibility* because it is unlikely that every aspect of your business will go exactly as planned. Prepare to adjust your budget to account for changes.

- You can *create a comprehensive budget that helps you manage your financial resources* effectively by taking into account factors such as revenue projections, fixed and variable expenses, contingency plans, and profit margins.

Regularly reviewing and updating your budget allows you to make necessary adjustments while maintaining control over the financial health of your startup. You'll be better prepared to navigate the challenges of bootstrapping and set your startup on the path to sustainable growth if you stick to a well-planned budget.

Tracking Expenses

Tracking and monitoring expenses is one of the most important aspects of managing your bootstrapped startup's finances. Keeping a close eye on your spending allows you to maintain control over your financial resources, identify cost-cutting opportunities, and ensure that you stay within your budget.

In this section, we'll emphasize the significance of tracking expenses and offer suggestions for tools and techniques to help you stay organized and keep accurate records.

- **The Value of Tracking Expenses:** Tracking expenses allows you to gain insights into the financial health of your startup, identify trends, and make informed decisions. You can quickly identify any deviations from your budget, pinpoint areas where you may be overspending, and adjust your spending habits by regularly monitoring your expenses. This proactive approach can save your startup from potential financial problems and help it succeed in the long run.

There are numerous tools and techniques to assist you in tracking & managing your expenses. Popular choices are:

- **Accounting software:** Programs such as QuickBooks, Xero, and FreshBooks provide comprehensive expense tracking features and can integrate with your bank accounts and credit cards, making it simple to stay organized and keep accurate records.

- **Spreadsheets:** For those who prefer a more hands-on approach, creating a customized expense tracking spreadsheet in Excel or Google Sheets can be a good way to keep track of your spending.

- **Apps for tracking expenses:** Expensify and Mint are mobile apps that can help you track your expenses on the go and sync them with your other financial management tools.

- **Keeping Organized:** Whatever tools you use, it's critical to stay organized and create a system for categorizing and documenting your expenses. Maintain a clear, easy-to-understand filing system and update your records on a regular basis to ensure consistency.

You'll be better equipped to make informed financial decisions, optimize your budget, and ensure the long-term success of your business if you closely monitor your spending and keep accurate records. Utilize the available tools and techniques to stay organized and in control of your startup's financial health.

Cash Flow Management

Cash flow management is an important aspect of running a bootstrapped startup because it directly affects the company's ability to meet financial obligations and invest in growth opportunities.

In this section, we'll define cash flow management and offer strategies for keeping a healthy cash flow in a bootstrapped startup, such as optimizing payment terms, lowering overhead, and managing inventory.

- **The Definition of Cash Flow Management:** Cash flow management refers to the process of monitoring, analyzing, and optimizing a company's cash inflows and outflows. It is critical for bootstrapped startups to keep enough cash on hand to cover expenses and invest in growth. Effective cash flow management assists businesses in anticipating potential cash shortages, making sound financial decisions, and maintaining financial stability.

- **Methods for Maintaining a Healthy Cash Flow:** There are several strategies that bootstrapped startups can use to keep their cash flow healthy:

- **Payment terms optimization:** Negotiate favorable payment terms with your clients and suppliers to ensure that you receive payments on time and do not overextend your payables. This can include giving clients early payment discounts or requesting longer payment terms from suppliers.

- **Reducing overhead:** Review your company's expenses on a regular basis and identify areas where you can cut costs without sacrificing the quality of your product or service. Contracts may need to be renegotiated, office space optimized, or non-essential expenses reduced.

- **Creating recurring revenue:** Create a recurring revenue model to ensure your company has consistent cash flow.

You can maintain a healthy cash flow that supports the financial stability and growth of your business by optimizing payment terms, reducing overhead, managing inventory, and generating recurring revenue. Monitoring and analyzing your cash flow on a regular basis will allow you to make informed decisions and ensure that your startup remains financially viable in the long run.

Cost-Cutting Strategies

Startups that are bootstrapped frequently operate on a tight budget, making it critical to identify and implement cost-cutting strategies that do not jeopardize the quality of the product or service being offered. You can save money while maintaining a high standard of quality by being resourceful and strategic.

- **Make use of technology:** Use automation tools and software to streamline operations and boost efficiency. This can help you save time, cut labor costs, and even improve output quality.

- *Consider contracting out non-core tasks to freelancers* or specialized service providers. This can assist you in lowering the overhead costs associated with full-time employees, such as office space and benefits.

- *Seek opportunities to collaborate with other businesses or professionals* who may be willing to exchange services or products, effectively lowering costs for both parties.

- **Negotiate better deals with suppliers:** Look for opportunities to negotiate better deals with suppliers, such as bulk order discounts or longer payment terms, which can help you manage your cash flow more effectively.

- *Reduce the size of your office* if possible, or consider remote work to save money on rent and utilities.

- *Reduce marketing expenses by utilizing low-cost marketing* channels such as social media and content marketing to reach your target audience without breaking the bank.

- **Monitor and control expenses:** Review your expenses on a regular basis to identify areas where savings can be made, and establish clear spending guidelines within your organization.

Implementing cost-cutting strategies in your bootstrapped startup can help you save resources while maintaining the quality of your product or service. You can create a lean and efficient operation that supports the growth and success of your business by focusing on areas such as technology, outsourcing, collaboration, negotiation, and expense management.

Financial Forecasting

For bootstrapped startups, financial forecasting is an essential component of financial planning. Entrepreneurs can make informed decisions about their business and develop strategies to ensure financial stability and growth by projecting future revenues, expenses, and cash flow.

To create accurate financial forecasts, begin by collecting historical financial data from your company, if it has it, or from similar businesses in your industry. This information can be used to identify trends and patterns that will help you make projections. Consider any external factors, such as market conditions, competition, and economic trends, that may have an impact on the financial performance of your startup in the future.

When making forecasts, be conservative in your estimates to account for unforeseen challenges and market fluctuations. Divide your forecasts into short-term (monthly or quarterly) and long-term (annual) projections to allow for changes based on actual performance and changing circumstances.

It is important to review and update your financial forecasts on a regular basis as new information becomes available. This will allow you to adjust your budget and decision-making processes accordingly, ensuring that your startup stays on track to meet its financial objectives.

Financial forecasting is an important tool for bootstrapped startups because it informs budgeting and decision-making processes. You can effectively manage your startup's finances and ensure its long-term viability and growth by developing realistic and conservative projections, reviewing and updating them on a regular basis, and using them to guide your financial strategies.

Break-Even Analysis

Break-Even Analysis: A critical financial tool for bootstrapped startups, the break-even analysis helps entrepreneurs understand when their business will begin to generate profits. By calculating and interpreting break-even points, you can assess your startup's financial viability and make informed decisions about pricing strategy, costs, and sales targets.

You must understand your fixed costs, variable costs, and revenue generated per unit sold in order to calculate the break-even point. When total revenue equals total costs, the break-even point is reached (fixed costs plus variable costs).

The break-even analysis formula is as follows:

Break-Even Point (in units) = Fixed Costs / (Revenue per Unit - Variable Cost per Unit)

Interpreting the break-even point can provide useful information about your company's operations. With fewer sales, your startup can cover its costs and start making a profit, making it more financially viable. A higher break-even point, on the other hand, indicates that you must sell more units before generating profits, which may necessitate additional effort and resources.

Changes in costs, pricing, and market conditions can all have an impact on your startup's financial viability, so it's critical to re-evaluate your break-even point on a regular basis. Continuously evaluating your break-even point will assist you in making informed decisions and adapting your business strategies to ensure long-term growth.

Break-even analysis is an important tool for determining a bootstrapped startup's financial viability. By calculating and interpreting break-even points, you can make informed decisions about pricing, costs, and sales targets, ensuring your company's financial stability and profitability. Reevaluating your break-even point on a regular basis will help you adapt to changing market conditions and maintain a sustainable growth trajectory.

Managing Debt and Credit

Debt and credit management are critical for bootstrapped startups because they can have a significant impact on the financial health and sustainability of the company. Entrepreneurs should focus on minimizing debt, using credit wisely, and maintaining a healthy credit score to effectively manage debt and credit.

Begin by reducing your debt as much as possible. Deferring non-essential purchases, negotiating better terms with suppliers, or consolidating existing debt into more manage-able terms may all be part of this strategy. When using credit, use it wisely by taking advantage of low interest rates and making timely payments to avoid paying extra interest and penalties.

Maintaining a healthy credit score is also critical, as it can determine your startup's future access to financing and favor-able credit terms. Regularly monitor your credit score and take steps to improve it, such as making on-time payments, keeping credit utilization low, and avoiding unnecessary credit inquiries.

Effective debt and credit management is critical for boot-strapped startups. You can ensure that your startup is finan-cially stable and has access to the resources it needs to grow and thrive by minimizing debt, using credit wisely, and main-taining a healthy credit score. Adopting a proactive approach to debt and credit management will benefit your company in the long run and position you for success.

Financial Reporting and Analysis

As a bootstrapped entrepreneur, knowing your startup's financial situation is critical for making sound decisions and ensuring long-term success. Regular financial reporting and analysis provide valuable insights into your company's finan-cial health, allowing you to track progress, identify potential problems, and take corrective action as needed.

Understanding key financial metrics is an important aspect of financial reporting and analysis. Profitability ratios, liquidity ratios, efficiency ratios, and solvency ratios are examples of these. Familiarizing yourself with these metrics and consistently tracking them can provide valuable insights into the performance and financial health of your business.

Consider using accounting software or other tools that can automate the process and generate comprehensive reports to make the most of financial reporting and analysis. These tools can assist you in tracking your financial metrics and identifying trends that may have an impact on your business. You can make more informed decisions about resource allocation, pricing, cost reduction, and overall business strategy by reviewing and analyzing your financial data on a regular basis.

For bootstrapped startups, regular financial reporting and analysis are essential. You can better manage your company's financial health and ensure its long-term success by understanding key financial metrics and using data to make informed business decisions. A proactive approach to financial reporting will allow you to stay ahead of potential issues and make strategic adjustments as needed, assisting your bootstrapped startup's overall growth and sustainability.

Preparing for Future Funding

Bootstrapped startups may require outside funding to accelerate growth, scale operations, or enter new markets. Effective budgeting and financial management practices are critical in positioning your startup for future funding opportunities, whether they are angel investments, venture capital, or loans.

First, keep accurate and up-to-date financial records to show potential investors your startup's financial health and stability. This transparency enables investors to assess the potential return on investment and understand your company's financial position.

Next, concentrate on increasing revenue and maintaining profitability, as these factors are appealing to investors seeking a high return on investment. A track record of consistent revenue growth and profitability demonstrates your startup's potential for future success.

Create a strong network within your industry and among potential investors. Networking can provide you with valuable insights, resources, and connections that can help you secure funding when the time comes.

Lastly, create a compelling pitch deck and business plan that highlights your startup's growth potential, market opportunity, and competitive advantages. These documents will be critical in presenting your case to potential investors and convincing them of your venture's viability.

By practicing effective budgeting and financial management, you can lay a strong foundation for your bootstrapped startup, making it more appealing to potential investors. Financial stability, profitability, and growth potential, as well as a compelling pitch deck and business plan, will significantly increase your chances of securing the funding required to take your startup to the next level.

6

BUILDING A MINIMUM VIABLE PRODUCT (MVP)

～

As a bootstrapped entrepreneur, I've learned how important it is to get a product or service into the hands of customers as soon as possible, even if it isn't fully developed or polished. This method allows you to test your assumptions, collect valuable feedback, and iterate on your offering all while earning money.

I recall a time when my company launched a new lead generation service. Rather than waiting for the service to be perfected, we started testing it right away, allowing us to make money and improve our offering based on real-world usage. In contrast, we once invested six months and significant resources in developing a CRM that was never released or received feedback from potential users. The disparity in outcomes between these two experiences was striking, emphasizing the importance of developing a Minimum Viable Product (MVP) and getting it in front of customers as soon as possible.

By the end of this chapter, you'll have a solid understanding of the MVP concept and how to apply it to your bootstrapped startup to maximize success and minimize waste.

Understanding the MVP Concept

Understanding the concept of a Minimum Viable Product (MVP) is important for bootstrapped startups. It refers to a simplified version of your product or service that includes only the core features required to address the needs and solve the pain points of your target customers. The goal of an MVP is to validate your startup idea, collect feedback from early adopters, and shorten time-to-market by focusing on the most important functionalities.

Creating an MVP allows bootstrapped entrepreneurs to market test their product or service without investing significant time and resources in developing a full-fledged version. You can assess market demand, learn from user feedback, and iterate on your product based on real-world data by launching an MVP. This method reduces the risk of failure while also ensuring that you're creating something that customers genuinely want and need.

For bootstrapped startups, the MVP idea is key to the product development process. You can validate your startup idea, learn from your target customers, and improve your product or service based on real-world feedback by creating an MVP. By adopting the MVP mindset, you can shorten your time-to-market, reduce risks, and create a product that truly addresses the needs and pain points of your target market.

Defining Your Core Features

Provide assistance in identifying the key features and functionalities of your product or service that directly address the needs and pain points of your target audience.

As a bootstrapped entrepreneur, you must prioritize the

development of your core product or service features. These are the elements that directly address the needs and pain points of your target audience, making them essential to the success of your startup.

Follow these steps to define your core features:

- **Reexamine your target market:** Review your target market analysis and customer profiles to remind yourself of your potential customers' specific needs and preferences.

- **Determine key pain points:** Determine the most pressing issues and challenges that your target audience faces and that your product or service aims to address.

- **Concentrate on value:** Determine which features of your product or service will provide the most value to your customers, effectively addressing their needs and pain points.

- *Rank the identified features* according to their importance to your target audience and the overall value they provide.

- **Verify with customers:** Seek feedback from prospective customers to validate your assumptions and ensure that the core features you've chosen are truly valuable and relevant.

- **Iterate and refine:** Be prepared to iterate and refine your core features in response to customer feedback and market trends to keep your product or service relevant and competitive.

You can maximize the value of your offering, optimize your development resources, and increase the likelihood of your startup's success by focusing on the essential features and functionalities that address the needs and pain points of your target audience.

Prioritizing Features

Prioritizing features for your MVP is vital because it directly impacts the success of your bootstrapped startup. Striking the right balance between providing value to your customers and keeping development costs and timelines manageable is critical for maximizing the potential of your startup.

It's essential to prioritize features that address your target customers' most pressing needs and pain points. This ensures that your MVP will be well received by your target audience and will encourage customer engagement. Overloading your MVP with features can result in higher costs, longer development times, and a potentially confusing user experience. Instead, prioritize the development of a core set of features that are both functional and valuable to your customers.

Iterate and improve your MVP in response to user feedback and data, gradually introducing new features and improvements as needed. This iterative approach enables you to make data-driven decisions while reducing the risk of investing in features that may not be appealing to your target audience.

You can build a product with a strong foundation for success by focusing on delivering value to your customers while managing development costs and timelines. Regularly assessing and adjusting feature priorities based on user feedback and data will allow you to optimize your offering and drive long-term growth for your startup.

Developing Your MVP on a Budget

Creating an MVP on a tight budget necessitates ingenuity and resourcefulness, but it is doable with the right strategies in place.

Here are pointers to help you build your MVP on a budget:

- **Make use of open-source tools:** Make use of free or low-cost open-source software and tools to help you build the foundation for your MVP. Open-source resources provide a low-cost way to gain access to valuable technology without making large upfront investments.

- **Platforms with no or low code should be used:** Non-technical founders can use no-code and low-code development platforms to create functional prototypes or even full-fledged applications with little coding knowledge. These platforms can drastically reduce the time and money required to create an MVP.

- **Outsource development work:** If you don't have the technical skills to build your MVP in-house, consider hiring freelancers or remote development teams. This allows you to gain access to skilled professionals at a lower cost than hiring full-time staff while maintaining control over your project.

- **Concentrate on core features:** When developing your MVP, focus on the core features that address the primary pain points of your target market. This allows you to create a functional product that can be tested and validated in the market without

investing in features that may or may not be
required at this stage.

- **Iterate and refine:** Once your MVP has been tested,
  collect feedback and use it to iterate and refine your
  product. This continuous improvement process will
  help you make the most of your limited budget by
  ensuring that your MVP evolves into a solution that
  truly meets the needs of your target audience.

Developing an MVP on a budget is possible by utilizing
open-source tools, utilizing no-code or low-code platforms,
outsourcing development work, focusing on core features,
and iterating based on user feedback. Using these strategies,
bootstrapped startups can create a viable product with
limited resources, allowing them to test their ideas in the
market and fine-tune their offerings to better meet the needs
of their customers.

Design and User Experience

A well-designed product interface can make or break your
product's or service's perception among users. In this section,
we will discuss how to create an intuitive and accessible
product interface.

Begin by researching the needs and preferences of your
target audience. This will assist you in understanding their
expectations and creating a design that meets their needs.
Conduct usability tests with prospective users to collect feedback and identify areas for improvement. If you lack the skills
or resources to create an engaging design yourself, consider
hiring a professional designer or using online design
resources.

Another important factor to consider is accessibility.
Follow established accessibility guidelines and best practices

to ensure that your product or service is accessible to users with disabilities. You demonstrate empathy and commitment to inclusivity by designing a user experience that meets the needs of all users.

Prioritizing a user-centered design and a consistent user experience for your MVP is key to your success. You can create an intuitive and accessible product interface that resonates with your users by researching the needs of your target audience, conducting usability tests, and focusing on accessibility. Remember that a well-designed product will not only attract users but will also contribute to your boot-strapped startup's overall positive perception.

Testing and Iteration

Continuous testing and iteration are critical components of the MVP development process in the world of bootstrapped startups. It is pivotal to collect and analyze user feedback in order to identify areas where your product or service can be improved. This allows you to make data-driven decisions and fine-tune your offering to ensure it meets the needs and expectations of your target audience.

Consider using tools like surveys, focus groups, or user interviews to effectively collect user feedback. Monitoring user behavior and engagement metrics can also provide useful information about how your target audience interacts with your MVP. Paying close attention to these data points allows you to spot patterns and trends that may indicate areas for improvement.

After you've gathered feedback and analyzed the data, use it to guide your decision-making. Prioritize the most significant pain points or areas for improvement in your MVP, and iterate on your product or service accordingly. Remember that iteration is an ongoing process, and testing and refining your offering on a regular basis will help you stay ahead of the competition and adapt to changing market conditions.

Continuous testing and iteration are major elements of the MVP development process. You can refine your product or service to better serve your target audience and drive business growth by collecting user feedback, identifying areas for improvement, and making data-driven decisions.

Launching Your MVP

After devoting time and resources to developing a minimum viable product (MVP) for your bootstrapped startup, it is essential that you efficiently launch it to your target audience. This will assist you in gathering useful user feedback, validating your concept, and refining your product or service offering.

Promoting your MVP via low-cost channels is critical for reaching your target audience while conserving your limited resources. Social media platforms like Facebook, Twitter, LinkedIn, and Instagram are great places to promote your MVP. You can raise awareness, generate interest, and encourage potential users to try your product by creating engaging content, sharing regular updates, and interacting with your audience.

Another effective tool for promoting your MVP is email marketing. Creating a mailing list of prospective customers and sending targeted, personalized emails can assist you in communicating the value of your product and driving traffic to your landing page. Consider collaborating with industry influencers and bloggers who can help spread the word about your MVP.

Content marketing, search engine optimization (SEO), and online forums or communities relevant to your target market are all low-cost ways to promote your MVP. You can effectively reach your target audience without breaking the bank by combining these promotional strategies.

Launching your MVP is a significant aspect in validating your startup concept and gathering valuable feedback from your target audience. You can effectively promote your MVP and increase its chances of success by utilizing cost-effective channels such as social media, email marketing, and content marketing. Remember to track the effectiveness of your marketing efforts and adjust your strategies as needed to make the best use of your limited resources.

Tracking Success Metrics

KPIs can help you identify areas for improvement or optimization by providing valuable insights into how well your product or service is performing.

Some important KPIs to monitor for your MVP include:

- Metrics such as daily active users, session duration, and time spent on specific features *can help you understand how users interact with your product* and which aspects are most appealing.

- **Conversion rates:** Measuring the percentage of users who complete a desired action, such as signing up for a trial, making a purchase, or upgrading to a premium plan, can help you evaluate and optimize the effectiveness of your sales funnel.

- **Customer satisfaction scores:** Gathering feedback from users via surveys or rating systems can provide insights into their overall satisfaction with your product and assist you in identifying areas for improvement.

- **Churn rate:** This metric represents the percentage of customers who stop using your product after a certain period of time. A high churn rate may indicate that users are not finding enough value in your product or that usability issues need to be addressed.

- **Customer acquisition cost (CAC):** Calculating the cost of acquiring a new customer allows you to assess the effectiveness of your marketing and sales efforts and identify areas for improvement.

Tracking success metrics via KPIs is key for understanding your MVP's performance and guiding your decision-making process for future iterations. You can identify strengths and weaknesses in your product, make informed decisions, and ultimately create a more successful offering by closely monitoring user engagement, conversion rates, customer satisfaction scores, churn rate, and customer acquisition cost.

Incorporating User Feedback

As you refine your MVP, focus on the enormous value of incorporating user feedback into your development process. You can identify areas for improvement, make necessary adjustments, and ensure that your product or service aligns with the needs and expectations of your target audience by actively engaging with them and obtaining their insights.

Consider conducting surveys, conducting interviews, or organizing focus groups with a diverse range of users to effectively solicit user feedback. To gain a comprehensive understanding of user experiences and preferences, use both qualitative and quantitative data. Use social media, online forums, and other digital platforms to solicit unsolicited feedback and monitor conversations about your product or service.

When analyzing user feedback, prioritize feedback that is relevant to the goals and objectives of your startup. Distinguish between subjective opinions and actionable insights by identifying recurring themes and patterns. Be open to criticism and welcome the opportunity to learn from your customers, as their input can help shape the success of your bootstrapped startup.

By actively soliciting, analyzing, and acting on user feedback, you can continuously improve your product or service, better align with the needs of your target market, and ultimately drive your company's growth and success.

Pivoting and Scaling

The process of testing and validating your MVP can provide valuable insights into your bootstrapped startup's market fit and potential. Being willing to pivot and scale your business in response to these results is critical for long-term success. In this section, we will discuss the importance of adaptability and offer advice on determining when it is time to make significant changes or scale your product for broader market adoption.

The ability to adapt and respond to feedback and market changes is an important part of being a successful bootstrapped entrepreneur. Making a strategic shift in your business model, product, or target market in response to new information, customer feedback, or market trends is referred to as pivoting. Scaling, on the other hand, entails growing your company in order to reach a larger audience and generate more revenue while maintaining or improving efficiency.

Examine the feedback from your MVP testing and validation process to determine when it's time to pivot or scale. Look for patterns and trends that indicate your current approach might not be optimal or that a different approach might produce better results. Monitor your key performance indicators (KPIs) as well to track your progress toward your goals and identify areas for improvement.

When contemplating a pivot, it is important to weigh the potential risks and benefits of the change. Make sure that any pivot is supported by data and customer insights, and be prepared to iterate on your new course as needed. Similarly, when scaling, make sure you have a solid foundation in place, which includes efficient processes, scalable infrastructure, and a clear understanding of your target market.

Finally, being willing to pivot and scale your bootstrapped startup in response to MVP testing and validation results is vital for long-term success. You can identify the right time to make significant changes or scale your product for broader market adoption by closely monitoring feedback, KPIs, and market trends. Embracing adaptability and learning from your mistakes will position your startup for long-term growth and success.

Following that, we'll proceed to Chapter 7: Low-Cost Marketing Strategies, where we'll look at various low-cost methods for promoting your bootstrapped startup and reaching your target audience.

7

LOW-COST MARKETING STRATEGIES

~

To get my product in front of my ideal customers in the early days of my first business, I had to rely on low-cost marketing strategies. I'd like to share a story about how I used these low-cost methods to make connections and grow my business.

Attending events and conferences where I knew my target audience would be present was an important part of my marketing strategy when we first started. I would network and build relationships with potential clients, which proved to be an effective way of spreading the word about my startup.

I started a niche-specific podcast and invited industry experts to share their stories and insights to further establish my presence in the industry. I published new episodes every week, without fail, which helped me establish authority and credibility in my field. The podcast also allowed me to connect with key industry players, some of whom became clients or referred others to my company.

In addition to the podcast, I used content marketing, social media, and strategic partnerships to build an email list of potential customers. With this list, I carefully crafted and dripped content that would provide value while keeping my startup at the forefront of my audience's minds.

One of the most effective marketing strategies I used was to rely on referrals from industry contacts. I was able to generate a steady stream of new business through word-of-mouth recommendations by providing exceptional service and nurturing relationships with existing clients.

In this chapter, we'll look at some low-cost marketing strategies you can use to promote your bootstrapped startup and reach your target audience. By utilizing these techniques, you can lay a solid foundation for your company and achieve long-term growth without breaking the bank.

Content Marketing

It is impossible to overestimate the importance of content marketing for bootstrapped startups. It is a low-cost method of attracting and engaging your target audience by providing them with useful, informative, and shareable content. You can establish your brand as a thought leader, build trust, and drive organic traffic to your website by creating high-quality content that resonates with your audience.

Focus on creating content that showcases your expertise and addresses the pain points of your target customers to create content on a budget. Determine which content formats are most effective for your audience, such as blog posts, infographics, videos, or podcasts, and prioritize those that require the least amount of investment. Use free or low-cost content creation tools, such as Canva for graphics or Anchor for podcasting. Consider repurposing existing content into new formats to broaden its reach and value.

Collaborate with industry influencers, guest bloggers, or other entrepreneurs to create useful content and increase your reach. This not only saves you time and money, but it also allows you to tap into their audience and credibility. Finally, to increase visibility and traffic, promote your content on relevant social media platforms, forums, and groups.

Content marketing is a proven strategy for bootstrapped startups looking to attract and engage their target audience on a limited budget. You can establish your brand's authority and drive organic growth without breaking the bank by focusing on creating valuable, informative, and shareable content, leveraging low-cost tools, and collaborating with others.

Social Media Marketing

Social media platforms have a substantial function in low-cost marketing because they provide a powerful way for bootstrapped startups to reach and engage potential customers without incurring significant costs. Channels such as Facebook, Twitter, LinkedIn, and Instagram, when used effectively, can greatly expand your brand's reach, drive website traffic, and generate leads.

To get the most out of social media marketing, stick to a posting schedule and share relevant, engaging content tailored to your target audience. This can include blog posts, videos, images, and industry news that highlight your knowledge and the worth of your product or service. Engaging with your audience through comments, messages, and shares can also help to build strong relationships and brand loyalty.

You can use social media analytics tools to track the performance of your content and identify areas for improvement. You can optimize your social media strategy to maximize reach and engagement by testing different types of content and posting times. Consider using social media platforms' targeted advertising options to reach specific audience segments that are most likely to convert.

To recap, social media marketing provides a priceless opportunity for bootstrapped startups to reach out to and engage with potential customers on a shoestring budget. You can use social media platforms like Facebook, Twitter, LinkedIn, and Instagram to drive brand awareness, customer acquisition, and business growth by creating and sharing relevant, engaging content, consistently interacting with your audience, and leveraging analytics tools.

Email Marketing

Email marketing is essential for developing relationships with your target audience, increasing engagement, and, ultimately, generating revenue for your bootstrapped startup. When done correctly, it can provide a high return on investment (ROI) while also assisting you in staying in touch with your customers and prospects.

Create an opt-in form on your website or landing page, encouraging visitors to subscribe to receive updates, promotions, or valuable content, to begin building and managing an email list. To increase the likelihood of subscription, provide incentives such as discounts or exclusive resources. To manage your list and ensure compliance with data protection regulations, use an email marketing platform such as Mailchimp or Sendinblue.

Focus on delivering relevant and valuable content that addresses the needs and interests of your target audience when creating email campaigns. Personalize your emails by using their names and segmenting your list to send targeted messages to different groups based on their preferences, behavior, or demographics. Pay close attention to the subject lines as well, as they play an important role in determining open rates. Try out different subject lines to see what works best for your audience.

Tracking the results of your email marketing campaigns is

absolutely essential, as are key metrics such as open rates, click-through rates, conversion rates, and unsubscribe rates. Analyzing these metrics will help you understand what works and what doesn't, allowing you to improve your email marketing strategy and refine your campaigns.

Email marketing is an effective tool for building relationships with your target audience, increasing engagement, and generating revenue in a bootstrapped startup. You can optimize your email marketing strategy and achieve greater success in your business endeavors by building and managing an email list, crafting targeted campaigns, and tracking results.

Search Engine Optimization (SEO)

Search Engine Optimization (SEO) is an essential online marketing strategy that focuses on increasing the visibility of your website in search engine results, driving organic traffic to your site, and ultimately increasing the exposure of your brand to potential customers. Effective SEO can be a game changer in generating leads and revenue without incurring significant marketing expenses for bootstrapped startups operating on a limited budget.

SEO entails optimizing the content, structure, and meta-data of your website so that search engines can easily crawl, index, and understand it. Using relevant keywords and phrases that your target audience is likely to search for, creating high-quality and engaging content, optimizing your site's structure and URLs, using descriptive and concise title tags and meta descriptions, and developing a strong backlink profile are all part of this process.

To get started with SEO, conduct keyword research to identify the terms and phrases your target audience is looking for, and then naturally incorporate them into your content. Concentrate on producing useful, engaging, and shareable content that will appeal to both your audience and search engines. Furthermore, make sure your website is user-friendly, with clear and concise navigation menus, clean URLs, and optimized images.

Furthermore, it is necessary to track and analyze your website's performance on a regular basis with tools like Google Analytics and Google Search Console, which provide invaluable insights into your site's traffic, user behavior, and search engine rankings. You can refine your SEO strategy and improve your website's search engine visibility by consistently tracking and analyzing your site's performance.

SEO is a valuable tool for bootstrapped startups looking to drive organic traffic and generate leads on a shoestring budget. You can significantly improve your startup's online presence and reach a wider audience by understanding the fundamentals of SEO and implementing best practices in content creation and website optimization. Regularly monitoring and analyzing the performance of your site will allow you to make informed decisions and continuously improve your SEO strategy to achieve even better results.

Public Relations and Media Outreach

Public relations and media outreach are essential to establishing buzz and increasing brand visibility for your bootstrapped startup. You can reach a larger audience, attract potential customers, and establish credibility in your industry by utilizing public relations strategies. The key to successful public relations efforts is to craft compelling press releases and pitches that highlight the unique aspects of your startup, as well as to cultivate relationships with journalists and influencers who can help amplify your message.

Focus on highlighting the newsworthy aspects of your startup, such as product launches, milestones, or industry innovations, when writing a compelling press release. To add credibility to your story, be concise, clear, and informative, and include relevant quotes from key team members. When pitching to journalists or influencers, do your homework and tailor your pitch to their specific interests or beat. This personalization demonstrates that you've done your research and increases your chances of obtaining coverage.

It takes time and effort to build relationships with journalists and influencers. Attend industry events, interact with them on social media, and add value by sharing relevant information or insights. This approach builds trust and rapport, increasing the likelihood that they will cover your startup in the future.

Public relations and media outreach can help your bootstrapped startup generate buzz and raise its visibility. You can improve your brand's image and attract new customers by writing compelling press releases and pitches and cultivating relationships with journalists and influencers. These efforts contribute to your startup's overall success and growth without requiring a significant financial investment.

Networking and Community Building

Networking and community building are integral factors of promoting your bootstrapped startup. You can create valuable opportunities for collaboration, knowledge sharing, and business growth by connecting with like-minded individuals, industry experts, and potential customers.

Attend industry events such as conferences, trade shows, and workshops to start networking. These gatherings are an excellent way to meet people in your industry and learn about the latest trends and innovations. Online forums and social media groups are also excellent resources for connecting with industry professionals and enthusiasts. Participate in discussions, share your thoughts, and demonstrate your expertise by making valuable contributions.

Local meetups are yet another effective method for expanding your network and community. Look for events and gatherings in your area that are related to the niche or target market of your startup. Attending these meetups allows you to make personal connections with others who share your interests and may be able to help your startup in a variety of ways.

Attending industry events, participating in online forums, and joining local meetups can help you build a network of contacts that will help your business grow. Building strong relationships with others in your field will not only help you promote your startup, but will also provide valuable insights, resources, and support for your entrepreneurial journey.

Influencer Marketing and Partnerships

When it comes to expanding your startup's reach, the power of influencer marketing and strategic partnerships cannot be overstated. You can tap into relevant influencers' and partners' established audiences and leverage their credibility to promote your product or service by collaborating with them.

Begin by identifying influencers and partners who share your target audience and share your brand values. Examine their content, demographics, and engagement levels to ensure they are a good fit for your startup. Personalize your approach when reaching out and concentrate on developing genuine, mutually beneficial relationships. Make your objectives and expectations clear, and provide influencers with the tools and resources they need to effectively promote your brand.

To motivate your partners and influencers, consider offering incentives such as exclusive discounts or commission-based earnings. Track and analyze the performance of your influencer marketing and partnership campaigns on a regular basis, and make changes as needed to maximize their effectiveness. Maintain open lines of communication with your partners and influencers, and be open to feedback and suggestions from them.

Influencer marketing and partnerships can be an effective tool for bootstrapped startups seeking to expand their reach and customer base. You can maximize the return on your investment and build long-lasting relationships by carefully selecting and collaborating with relevant influencers and partners.

Referral and Affiliate Programs

Referral and affiliate programs are effective low-cost marketing strategies that can help bootstrapped businesses attract new customers without breaking the bank. These programs encourage existing customers and partners to spread the word about your product or service by leveraging their networks and relationships.

Begin by identifying your target audience and the types of partners who can best reach them in order to successfully implement a referral or affiliate program. Create a clear and appealing incentive structure that will motivate both referrers and new customers. Make sure you have a streamlined tracking and attribution system in place to monitor program performance and reward partners appropriately.

Communication is another serious aspect of running a referral or affiliate program. Keep your partners up to date on updates, promotions, and best practices to ensure their success in promoting your company. Be open to their feedback and iterate on your program as needed, refining and optimizing it to achieve the best results.

Referral and affiliate programs can be extremely effective low-cost marketing strategies for bootstrapped businesses. Without a significant financial investment, you can encourage word-of-mouth promotion, drive new customers, and grow your business by carefully planning, implementing, and managing these programs. These strategies are especially beneficial for bootstrapped startups that must maximize limited resources while still achieving growth and success.

Guerilla Marketing Tactics

Guerilla marketing is a novel strategy that enables boot-strapped firms to generate buzz and attract attention on a shoestring budget. Startups can build interest and word-of-mouth promotion without spending a lot of money on traditional advertising by employing unusual approaches.

Among the successful guerilla marketing strategies are:

- *Ambient marketing entails placing advertisements or promotional materials in unexpected places,* such as sidewalks, park benches, or public transportation, in order to capture the attention of passers-by.

- **Stunt marketing:** Putting on a startling or eye-catching event in a public place can create a memorable experience and build discussion about your firm.

- *Shareable material, such as compelling films or social media challenges, can inspire* users to promote your message and gain organic exposure.

- **Collaboration marketing:** Collaborating with other startups or local businesses can help you combine resources, broaden your reach, and generate one-of-a-kind promotional possibilities.

- Connecting with your target audience through
  *community events, local meetups, or online forums
  can help you establish a loyal following* and foster
  genuine connections with potential clients.

The Dollar Shave Club's viral video, which jokingly intro-
duced their budget razor subscription service, is an example
of a successful guerrilla marketing campaign. With a small
marketing expenditure, the video received millions of views
and considerably increased the company's customer base.

Guerrilla marketing strategies allow bootstrapped firms to
generate buzz and attract attention without breaking the
bank. Startups may build unique experiences that engage
with their target audience and generate organic growth by
thinking outside the box and employing unusual tactics.

Tracking and Analyzing Results

As a bootstrapped startup, maximizing the return on investment (ROI) for your marketing efforts is top priority. To do so,
you must track and analyze the results of your campaigns in
order to determine their effectiveness. You can determine
which methods are producing the best results and optimize
your campaigns for maximum impact by measuring the
performance of your marketing strategies.

Set clear goals and key performance indicators (KPIs) for
each marketing initiative to get started. Website traffic,
conversion rates, social media engagement, and lead generation are examples of these metrics. Track and measure these
KPIs using tools like Google Analytics, social media analytics,
and email marketing software.

Following that, review and analyze the collected data on a
regular basis to identify trends, patterns, and areas for
improvement. Look for marketing channels that are generating the most engagement and conversions, and then opti-

mize your strategies to maximize those results. Also, be prepared to adjust or abandon underperforming campaigns in order to save money and time.

Don't be afraid to try out new marketing strategies or channels. Your marketing strategies should evolve alongside your startup. Continuously testing and refining your approach will ensure that you stay ahead of the competition and reach your target audience effectively.

You can ensure maximum impact and ROI by monitoring the performance of your campaigns and using data-driven insights to optimize your strategies. This strategy will allow you to wisely allocate your limited marketing resources, making the most of every dollar spent.

Now that we've covered low-cost marketing strategies, let's move on to Chapter 8: Networking and Relationship Building, where we'll talk about the importance of making strong connections within your industry and the value these connections can bring to your startup.

8

NETWORKING AND BUILDING RELATIONSHIPS

~

When I first started my entrepreneurial path, I rapidly recognized the value of networking and relationship development. My network was small, and I understood that connecting with the proper people could make or break the success of my startup. I reached out to educated, powerful persons in my niche using different channels, including Facebook, LinkedIn, email, phone calls, and text messaging, with the goal of increasing my network.

I made it a point to seek business advice from people in my industry, whether they were clients, influencers, friends, or competitors. I made an honest attempt to remain in touch and form true relationships with these people. With these relationships, I not only got useful insights, but I also developed a support system that proved invaluable throughout my journey.

I also sought out mentors in the industry I was servicing and reached out to other marketing company owners, asking for their advice and assistance. Surprisingly, most people were eager to offer their experiences and information. They wanted to give back and help to the development of others, which I greatly admired.

In this chapter, we will discuss the significance of networking and relationship building for bootstrapped firms. We'll talk about how to broaden your network, cultivate strong connections, and use these connections to grow your business.

By the end, you'll have a greater grasp of the importance of networking and relationship building in the world of boot-strapped businesses, as well as the skills required to build and maintain a strong, supportive network.

The Importance of Networking

Networking is a valuable trait for entrepreneurs, especially those who are bootstrapping their businesses. Connecting with other professionals, industry experts, and possible part-ners can provide useful insights into your market, identify new opportunities, and strengthen your support network while you negotiate the hurdles of growing your business.

Attending industry events, participating in online forums and groups, and participating in local business organizations are all ways to broaden your network. When meeting new people, it's imperative to be honest, show interest in their work, and provide assistance where possible. Strong relation-ships require two-way communication, and genuine connec-tions are more likely to result in mutually beneficial collaborations and referrals.

Furthermore, networking can lead to possible clients, mentors, and investors who can help your firm succeed. These connections are especially important for bootstrapped companies since they can provide access to resources and opportunities that would otherwise be inaccessible.

Networking is vital for the development and longevity of

a bootstrapped firm. You can get useful insights, discover new opportunities, and establish a strong support system by actively engaging with others in your sector and beyond. Genuine contacts and an open-minded approach to networking will ultimately help your firm and boost your entrepreneurial journey.

Identifying Your Networking Goals

Setting specific goals for your networking efforts can guarantee that your time and energy are wisely spent and directed toward obtaining real results. Defining your networking objectives will allow you to focus on the most valuable relationships and interactions, which will eventually lead to possible partners, clients, mentors, or investors.

Begin by identifying the exact goals you want to attain through networking. For example, you might wish to look for strategic partners to help you scale your business, interact with potential clients to validate your product or service offering, or seek assistance from experienced mentors who can provide significant insights and recommendations. Furthermore, networking can help you find potential investors who may be interested in financially helping your firm.

After you've set your networking objectives, prioritize them according to your startup's present needs and objectives. This will assist you in identifying the most appropriate events, forums, or online groups to join and participate in. By focusing on your top priorities, you can maximize the return on your networking efforts and make the most of your limited resources.

For a bootstrapped entrepreneur trying to create important contacts and connections, setting explicit networking goals is necessary. By establishing and prioritizing your objectives based on the needs of your firm, you may focus your networking efforts on the most impactful activities, ultimately leading to possible partners, consumers, mentors, or investors who can contribute to the growth and success of your startup.

Attending Industry Events

Identifying and attending industry events, conferences, and workshops is an effective approach to broaden your network and obtain important company insights. These events bring together experts from all backgrounds, providing one-of-a-kind opportunity to meet possible partners, consumers, investors, and mentors. Furthermore, they frequently include instructive seminars and lectures that can keep you up to date on the newest trends and advancements in your sector.

To get the most out of these events, do your homework ahead of time and pick the ones that are most relevant to your startup. Prepare an elevator pitch, make clear targets for the number of individuals you want to meet with, and follow up with new contacts as soon as possible after the event to maximize your networking prospects.

In addition, be an active participant by asking questions during panel discussions, conversing during breaks, and attending workshops or training sessions. This not only helps you learn more, but it also reflects your dedication to your profession and enthusiasm to learn.

Finally, attending industry events, conferences, and workshops is a significant factor of networking and relationship building for bootstrapped firms. These events provide great opportunity to broaden your network, get market insights, and keep current on industry trends. By actively participating and following up with new connections, you may develop your professional relationships and lay a firm foundation for the growth and success of your startup.

Building an Online Presence

In today's digital age, having a good online presence is fundamental for every startup's success, especially for bootstrapped enterprises that rely on organic visibility and word-of-mouth marketing. A strong online presence not only allows you to reach a larger audience, but it also builds your brand's credibility and authority in your industry.

Create a professional website that highlights your product or service offering to begin developing an effective online presence. To maximize visibility, your website should be user-friendly, visually appealing, and search engine optimized. Including a blog that shares important content relating to your sector as well, as this can assist position you as an expert in your field.

Another essential element of your internet presence is your social media platforms. Concentrate on popular sites among your target demographic and actively engage with them by sharing relevant material, reacting to comments, and participating in conversations. Creating a brand community can lead to improved client loyalty and organic growth.

Participate in relevant online forums and groups where your target audience is present. You may establish yourself as a skilled and trustworthy resource in your business by participating in discussions, providing helpful advice, and answering inquiries.

Having a strong internet presence is necessary for bootstrapped businesses since it helps develop credibility, authority, and trust. You may effectively increase your reach, engage with your target audience, and develop long-lasting relationships by investing time and effort in creating a professional website, keeping active social media profiles, and participating in online forums and communities.

Developing Your Personal Brand

For bootstrapped entrepreneurs looking to build a name for themselves in their field and acquire significant connections, developing a strong personal brand is key. Your personal brand is the sum of your experience, values, and distinct point of view, and it can be a strong tool for distinguishing yourself from competitors and gaining trust with your target audience.

Begin by defining your skills and areas of expertise, and then create a consistent messaging that highlights your distinct value proposition. This can contain your story, your vision, and the problems you are deeply committed to fixing. Make sure your online presence, including your website, social media profiles, and any material you publish, reflects your unique brand.

Provide great information and insights with your audience on a regular basis, establishing yourself as an industry expert and thought leader. Interact with individuals in your business, participate in debates, and attend events where you can share your knowledge and network.

Be sincere and loyal to your values at all times, as this will allow you to make genuine connections with those who share your message. Remember that developing a personal brand is an ongoing process that involves attention and commitment, so be prepared to devote time and effort in nurturing and changing your brand as your career progresses.

Creating a personal brand is a strategic technique for differentiating yourself in your sector and acquiring significant contacts. You may distinguish yourself from competition and develop trust with your target audience by demonstrating your skills, values, and distinct perspective. Engaging with others and offering valuable information on a regular basis can help you cement your position as an industry expert and thought leader, allowing you to build a strong network that will support the growth and success of your boot-strapped firm.

Mastering the Art of Conversation

Engaging in conversations effectively during networking events and online contacts is a necessary skill for boot-strapped entrepreneurs. You can form great relationships, create chances for collaboration, and produce significant leads by mastering the art of communication.

Active listening is an important part of good communication. Active listening shows genuine interest in the other person's views and opinions, which builds trust and connection. Maintain eye contact, nod in agreement, and make verbal affirmations to demonstrate that you are fully involved.

Another great method to stimulate discourse is to ask open-ended questions. You invite the other person to share their views and experiences by asking questions that need more than a simple "yes" or "no" answer. This promotes a deeper connection and meaningful communication.

Finding common ground is essential for developing rapport and long-term connections. Search for common interests, experiences, or issues that you can discuss to form a bond. This can assist you in standing out and being remembered by the individuals you meet.

Mastering the art of communication is a necessary ability for effective networking and relationship-building. You can engage in meaningful conversations that lead to significant relationships and possibilities by practicing active listening, asking open-ended questions, and identifying common ground. Remember that genuine connection and empathy go a long way toward creating and strengthening business relationships.

Building Genuine Relationships

In order to cultivate trust, provide value, and maintain regular communication, emphasize the importance of developing true, long-lasting connections rather than simply accumulating contacts.

Genuine connections are necessary for networking and establishing a successful bootstrapped firm. Rather of merely building a list of contacts, concentrate on cultivating genuine connections with people who share your values, ambitions, and interests. This strategy will not only result in more enjoyable and productive interactions, but it will also provide the groundwork for future collaborations and partnerships.

Be honest, upfront, and dependable in your relationships to build trust. Demonstrate real interest in others, actively listen to their concerns, and engage in meaningful conversations. You can build a good rapport with your network by displaying empathy and understanding.

In each connection, providing value is necessary. To indicate your want to help and support others, offer assistance, share ideas, or connect others with relevant possibilities. You will become an integral member of your network if you are a helpful resource, and others will be more eager to reciprocate your efforts.

Regular interaction is necessary for nurturing relationships over time. Maintain communication with your contacts via emails, phone conversations, or social media messaging. To keep connected and active with your network, make an effort to attend industry events, conferences, and meetups.

The key to effective networking in the realm of bootstrapped companies is the development of meaningful relationships. You may build strong, long-lasting connections that will contribute to the growth and success of your startup by fostering trust, giving value, and keeping regular communication.

Leveraging Your Existing Network

One of the most valuable things you have as a bootstrapped entrepreneur is your existing network of friends, family, colleagues, and acquaintances. By tapping into this network, you can identify prospective possibilities, contacts, and resources that can help your startup without spending a lot of time or money.

Make a list of everyone you know who might have experience, knowledge, or connections related to your business or target market. Contact these people and inform them about your new venture. When discussing your business, be sincere and upfront, and ask for their advise or if they know anyone who may assist you. Remember that individuals are typically willing to help those they know and trust, so don't be afraid to ask for help.

Attending business events, conferences, or local meetings is another efficient approach to expand your network. These events can provide valuable opportunity to network with like-minded people, potential clients, and industry professionals who can provide guidance and support. Also, don't underestimate the value of social media platforms such as LinkedIn, Twitter, or Facebook groups for expanding your network and making new connections in your field.

Always keep in mind that networking is a two-way street. When you expand your existing network and develop new relationships, remember to reciprocate by contributing your own expertise, experience, or resources as needed. This will not only strengthen your relationships, but will also position you as an important member of your industry and community.

Leveraging your existing network is a low-cost and effective approach to find chances, contacts, and resources for your bootstrapped firm. By being real, transparent, and aggressive in your approach, you may maximize your network and build long-term partnerships that will benefit your organization.

Following Up and Staying Connected

Following up after networking events and encounters is essential to developing and keeping professional ties, and it cannot be underestimated. You can develop these ties and build a strong network that will help your bootstrapped firm grow and prosper by making an effort to keep connected.

Regular communication with your network is one of the finest methods to stay connected with them. Call out to people you met at events or through introductions and thank them for their time and insights. Write individual notes, mentioning specific conversations or offering to assist them in any way you can.

Another strategy for cultivating these ties is to provide updates on your startup's growth, milestones, or any pertinent news. Sharing your triumphs and problems can foster a sense of community and motivate others to do the same. Also, provide important resources such as articles, industry reports, or tools that your contacts may find beneficial. This not only demonstrates that you are considering their needs, but it also places you as a valued resource in their network.

Use social media services like LinkedIn to stay in touch with your network. Interact with them, support their abilities, and participate in their material by like, commenting on, or sharing their postings. This shows your continued interest in their professional lives and develops a sense of community.

For bootstrapped entrepreneurs who want to develop strong, long-lasting professional relationships, following up and remaining engaged with your network is essential. Frequent communication, offering updates and relevant resources, and social media engagement are all excellent strategies to foster these connections. By putting time and effort into nurturing these relationships, you may build a supportive network that will help your startup grow and succeed.

The Power of Mentorship

Mentoring can be a great resource for bootstrapped entrepreneurs since experienced mentors can provide unique insights and advice obtained from their own experiences. These connections can assist you in navigating the difficulties of running a bootstrapped firm, making educated decisions, and avoiding frequent errors. You may expedite your learning curve, improve your problem-solving skills, and ultimately raise your chances of success by exploiting your mentors' knowledge and experience.

Consider visiting industry events, joining online networks, and engaging in startup accelerators or mentorship programs to discover and connect with mentors. When approaching possible mentors, be honest, courteous, and eager to learn from their experiences. Maintain open channels of contact and remember to express gratitude for their advice and assistance.

In conclusion, mentorship can be a valuable resource for bootstrapped entrepreneurs, giving valuable direction, counsel, and support throughout the business process. By seeking out and developing relationships with experienced mentors, you can have access to vital insights and expertise that can assist you in navigating the hurdles of running a bootstrapped firm, making smarter decisions, and ultimately increasing your chances of success.

9

OUTSOURCING AND HIRING ON A SHOESTRING

W hen I initially launched my marketing company, we concentrated on web design and development services. I spent numerous hours researching hundreds of companies before contacting those I felt created the greatest and most innovative work. Ultimately, I reached an agreement with one of the agencies to white label their work at first, allowing me to focus on marketing our services.

This agency's owner not only collaborated with me, but also mentored me in different elements of the business, including proposals, presentations, processes, project management, and pricing strategies. This relationship was a priceless learning experience that helped my company develop more efficiently.

To broaden our capabilities, I employed part-time video editors, copywriters, and graphic designers and paid them hourly. I took home less money than I should have at first, but this sacrifice allowed the business to develop and eventually become more profitable.

This personal story illustrates how bootstrapped firms can successfully outsource and hire on a minimal budget. You can not only save money by leveraging strategic alliances and outsourcing some duties, but you can also profit from the expertise of seasoned individuals. In the parts that follow, we will go through several tactics and concerns for outsourcing and hiring on a tight budget.

The Benefits of Outsourcing

For bootstrapped firms aiming to optimize resources while lowering expenses, outsourcing can be a game changer. Outsourcing has various benefits that can greatly effect your company's growth and profitability.

The potential cost savings is one of the most significant advantages of outsourcing. Outsourcing allows bootstrapped firms to obtain specialized talents and knowledge without incurring the financial burden of hiring full-time staff. This strategy can help you save money on salary, benefits, and office space while still delivering the support your company need.

Another benefit of outsourcing is its adaptability. Your demands may vary as your startup develops and changes, and outsourcing allows you to scale your resources up or down accordingly. This agility can help you respond to market developments and business issues more efficiently, ensuring that you always have the proper level of support.

An additional and substantial advantage of outsourcing is access to specialized talents and knowledge. By collaborating with third-party service providers, you can access a huge pool of talent that may not be available in your immediate network. Having access to specialist knowledge can assist you in filling skill gaps in your staff, ensuring that your business has the competence required to prosper in your industry.

Outsourcing provides various advantages to bootstrapped

businesses, including cost savings, flexibility, and access to specialized skills and knowledge. By properly employing outsourcing, you may optimize your resources and drive your business's growth while preserving financial control.

Identifying Tasks to Outsource

Outsourcing specific work to bootstrapped businesses can be a cost-effective approach to gain access to specialized talents and resources that are not available in-house. By determining which jobs to outsource, you can focus your team's efforts on core operations and maximize the growth potential of your firm.

Consider the following factors when determining which tasks are acceptable for outsourcing:

- **Non-core activities:** Begin by identifying tasks that are not critical to the core skills of your startup. They are often administrative or support duties that, while required, do not immediately add to the distinctive value proposition of your startup.

- **Specialty skills:** Determine whether there are any tasks that require specialist abilities that your team lacks. Outsourcing these services may be more efficient and cost-effective than developing these talents in-house or hiring full-time personnel with the necessary experience.

- **Time-consuming chores:** Consider tasks that take a large amount of time but do not necessarily provide significant value to your startup. Outsourcing these chores can provide your staff more time to focus on higher-impact operations.

- **Scalability:** Decide whether any tasks should be scaled up or down in response to swings in demand or business growth. Outsourcing can give the necessary flexibility to meet these changes without putting more strain on your team or incurring additional costs.

- **Cost-benefit analysis:** Do a cost-benefit analysis to evaluate the costs of outsourcing a work to the expenses of managing it internally. Outsourcing may be a realistic alternative for your startup if it proves to be more cost-effective.

Outsourcing can be a helpful option for bootstrapped businesses since it allows you to focus on your core capabilities while gaining access to specialized talents and resources that you may not have in-house. You may enhance your team's efficiency, effectively control costs, and drive the growth of your firm by carefully choosing which jobs to outsource.

Finding Reliable Freelancers and Contractors

Hiring trustworthy freelancers and contractors is key for bootstrapped businesses because they bring essential skills and knowledge without the commitment of full-time staff. Platforms like as Upwork, Fiverr, and Freelancer.com, which offer a variety of services and expertise across multiple industries, can be used to find and vet competent employees.

When using these platforms, it is imperative to carefully analyze potential applicants' profiles, portfolios, and evaluations in order to assess their talents, expertise, and dependability. Consider conducting interviews and asking samples of their work to determine their fit for your specific requirements. While working with freelancers and contractors, keep in mind that communication is essential, so make sure they are responsive and open to feedback.

Personal networks and referrals, in addition to online channels, can be key sources of talent. Ask for referrals from your professional network, coworkers, and friends. Individuals who have had firsthand experience working with freelancers and contractors may give you useful information about their work ethic, dependability, and skill level.

Locating trustworthy freelancers and contractors is important for bootstrapped firms seeking to leverage their resources and experience. Use platforms such as Upwork, Fiverr, and Freelancer.com, as well as personal networks and recommendations, to find competent professionals that can contribute to the success of your business. You may develop a productive and cost-effective working relationship with freelancers and contractors by carefully screening individuals and keeping open communication.

Creating Clear Project Descriptions

It is essential at a bootstrapped firm to make the most of your limited resources by successfully engaging with freelancers and contractors. This begins with writing detailed project descriptions that explain the scope, needs, and expectations of the work to be done. A well-written project description assists potential freelancers and contractors in understanding the project objectives, deliverables, and timescales, allowing them to appropriately assess their suitability for the task.

Make sure to include the following parts in your project description:

- A succinct title that conveys the purpose of the project effectively.

- A brief description of the project's purpose and goals.

- A precise description of the tasks and obligations that the freelancer or contractor must perform.

- Any technical or skill requirements required to perform the project.

- The anticipated completion timeline, including any milestones or deadlines.

- The project's budget or payment system.

- Any additional information or context that can assist prospective freelancers and contractors in better understanding the job.

By offering a detailed project description, you not only attract the ideal candidates but also provide the groundwork for a successful cooperation. This can help you prevent misunderstandings, delays, and additional costs that could impede the progress of your bootstrapped firm.

Thorough project descriptions are essential for effective communication with freelancers and contractors. You can ensure that your startup's projects are done efficiently and to a high degree by establishing the scope, needs, and expectations of the job, while also making the most of your limited resources. Concise project descriptions are an essential tool for a bootstrapped startup's effective outsourcing and hiring.

Establishing Effective Communication

Setting up clear channels of communication is one of the most important components of managing a remote workforce. This is especially important in a bootstrapped startup, because every team member's contribution is fundamental to the company's success. To begin, choose communication options that are suited for your team's needs and interests. There are several platforms available that promote real-time communication and collaboration, such as Slack, Microsoft Teams, or Google Meet.

Following that, schedule regular check-ins with your remote team members. Depending on the nature of the projects and the level of collaboration necessary, they can be daily, weekly, or bi-weekly. Check-ins can be formal meetings or casual touchpoints, but the goal is to keep consistent communication to ensure everyone is on the same page and things are moving along smoothly. It is also critical to foster an open and friendly environment in which team members may freely share their ideas, concerns, and issues. To create trust and teamwork, encourage open communication and provide constructive feedback.

Consider using project management tools such as Trello, Asana, or Basecamp to improve collaboration even further. These platforms enable team members to collaborate and exchange updates while tracking tasks, deadlines, and project progress. By centralizing project information, everyone can stay informed and on the same page.

While managing a remote workforce, especially in a bootstrapped startup, excellent interaction is essential. You can assure easy collaboration and project development by using proper communication methods, scheduling regular check-ins, encouraging open discourse, and leveraging project management platforms. Finally, this will help your bootstrapped startup's overall success and growth.

Managing and Monitoring Progress

Using project management tools and techniques allows you to keep track of work, set deadlines, and ensure deliverables are done on time and on budget. You can make informed judgments, deploy resources efficiently, and increase productivity if you have a clear picture of your startup's progress.

Project management solutions range from simple task management apps to more complicated platforms with extensive capabilities such as time monitoring, resource allocation, and reporting. Trello, Asana, and Basecamp are some popular possibilities. Consider your startup's specific needs, the size of your staff, and the complexity of your projects before choosing a tool. Remember that many project management solutions provide free or low-cost plans aimed for small organizations and startups.

Aside from the tools, establishing a clear project management methodology is necessary. Setting goals and objectives, assigning roles and responsibilities, developing timetables, and establishing communication protocols should all be part of this process. Frequently monitoring progress and changing plans as appropriate can keep your team on track and ready to adapt to any changes or obstacles that may arise.

You can successfully track progress, set deadlines, and manage deliverables by leveraging project management tools and methods, ensuring that your projects stay on schedule and under budget. Constantly evaluating and revising your plans will allow you to make informed decisions, manage resources efficiently, and maximize productivity, all while keeping financial discipline and assisting your startup's growth.

Hiring Interns and Entry-Level Talent

It is imperative to optimize available resources while keeping expenses low. Hiring interns or entry-level talent is one approach to achieve this. These employees frequently bring with them a fresh viewpoint and a strong desire to learn and grow within your organization. In this section, we will examine the advantages of employing interns and entry-level employees, as well as advice for identifying motivated, talented applicants willing to contribute to the success of your firm.

Hiring interns and entry-level employees has various advantages. For starters, they are often less expensive than seasoned professionals, allowing you to keep expenditures under control while still expanding your workforce. Furthermore, because these people are often eager to learn and progress, they will be more open to training and development opportunities. This can result in a more adaptable and flexible staff, making it easier for your firm to pivot and adjust to changing market conditions.

Consider collaborating with local universities, colleges, and trade schools to locate motivated, bright people. These colleges frequently have internship programs or job boards where you can meet possible applicants. Furthermore, social media platforms such as LinkedIn can be a helpful resource for locating entry-level talent looking for work. Make an interesting job description that stresses the opportunity for growth and learning within your firm to attract ambitious people wanting to make a difference.

Offering attractive bonuses and benefits is another suggestion for attracting excellent interns and entry-level employees. While you may not be able to compete on pay with larger corporations, you can provide a flexible work environment, opportunities for professional development, and a great company culture. For individuals trying to build a name for themselves in their chosen area, these characteristics might be just as appealing as a bigger pay.

Finally, employing interns and entry-level personnel might be a cost-effective and strategic method to expand the staff of your bootstrapped firm. You can develop a flexible and adaptable workforce that helps to the success of your startup by capitalizing on the energy and fresh views these employees bring. Remember to use educational institutions, social media platforms, and appealing job descriptions to discover qualified people, and to provide competitive perks and benefits to attract and retain top employees.

Building a Positive Company Culture

A strong company culture not only helps to retain talent, but it also fosters a sense of unity and collaboration among team members.

Hosting virtual team-building events is one method to foster a strong workplace culture. These events might range from a simple virtual coffee break to a more structured team session. The idea is to encourage team members to connect with one another, share their experiences, and form relationships outside of the confines of the traditional work environment.

Celebrating the accomplishments of your remote team members is another essential element of creating a positive business culture. Recognizing their contributions and applauding their triumphs can inspire pride and inspiration in your team. To keep your team interested and motivated, make sure to provide constructive comments and praise great achievement.

Maintaining a strong organizational culture also requires consistent communication. Frequent check-ins, team meetings, and one-on-one sessions can help to ensure that everyone is on the same page with the company's goals and feels included in decision-making. Promote open communication and give avenues for team members to express their concerns or thoughts.

Developing a positive corporate culture in a bootstrapped business needs purposeful effort and attention. You can create an environment where your remote team members feel valued and connected by conducting virtual team-building events, acknowledging milestones, and keeping open communication, eventually driving the success of your firm.

Navigating Legal and Compliance Issues

It is essential that you recognize and comply with relevant rules, regulations, and tax obligations when outsourcing and hiring remote workers in your bootstrapped firm. Failure to follow these recommendations may result in legal and financial implications that are harmful to the growth and reputation of your startup.

To effectively manage legal and compliance challenges, first understand the rules and regulations in the nations and jurisdictions where you intend to outsource or recruit remote workers. Understanding employment laws, tax requirements, and data privacy standards are all part of this. To assure your startup's compliance, consider speaking with legal and tax professionals that are well-versed in the jurisdictions involved.

Contractual arrangements with your outsourced workers or remote staff are another factor to consider. Contracts should explicitly explain the terms and circumstances of the working relationship, including intellectual property rights, confidentiality agreements, and termination clauses. Periodically examine and amend these contracts to ensure they are in accordance with any regulatory changes.

When recruiting remote workers, keep cultural differences and communication styles in mind, as these might have an impact on work relationships and productivity. To build a happy and productive work atmosphere, encourage open communication, establish clear expectations, and be culturally aware.

Overcoming legal and compliance challenges while outsourcing and hiring remote workers is necessary for your bootstrapped startup's long-term success. You can reduce potential risks and build a firm foundation for your organization by understanding and following to appropriate laws, regulations, and tax obligations. To ensure a seamless and compliant outsourcing and remote recruiting process, engage with legal and tax advisors, maintain clear contractual agreements, and promote open communication.

Scaling Your Team Responsibly

It is important to scale your staff ethically and sustainably, while keeping financial limits, company growth, and your startup's ongoing demands in mind. Expansion of your workforce too soon might result in excessive expenses and financial instability, but understaffing your organization can result in inefficiencies and stifle growth.

To scale your team responsibly, first assess your existing workload, team skills, and areas where you require additional experience. Prioritize hiring for roles that will have the most impact on your company's growth, and make sure that the additional costs are justified by the value they will bring to the startup.

Another big element of safe scaling is having the required infrastructure and resources in place to support your team's development. This includes providing the necessary tools, software, and equipment, as well as fostering a productive and collaborative work atmosphere.

Consider adopting flexible recruiting choices like as part-time employees, freelancers, or remote workers to keep your overhead low and your staff agile. This allows you to simply modify your staff structure to changing business needs without incurring exorbitant costs.

Scaling your team properly is necessary for your bootstrapped startup's long-term success. You may strike the appropriate balance between expanding your staff and keeping financial stability by carefully assessing your needs, prioritizing important recruits, and leveraging flexible hiring choices. Always keep an eye on the impact of your employment decisions on overall business performance and change your plan as necessary.

10

LEAN OPERATIONS AND PROCESS OPTIMIZATION

∽

W hen I first started my lead generation startup, I learned the value of building and refining processes as I went. Our approach was a little sloppy at first, but we recognized the need to streamline our operations and continually refine them for increased efficiency.

We realized as we grew that we couldn't create processes for things that didn't yet exist, so we shifted our focus to developing processes that were scalable and adaptable to our changing business needs. We hoped to develop a rinse-and-repeat strategy that would allow us to add new components as our company grew.

One of the most important aspects of our expansion has been the use of automation in as many areas as possible. We were able to streamline our operations, reduce the risk of human error, and save valuable time and resources by leveraging technology. This approach enabled us to work smarter, not harder, and laid the groundwork for our company's expansion.

Our company also prioritized personal and professional growth as one of our core values. Because we were committed to continuous improvement, we were constantly looking for ways to optimize and improve our processes. As we developed our SOPs, we discovered that the key to building a scalable company is constant process refinement and optimization.

Understanding Lean Principles

Although lean principles originated in the manufacturing industry, their concepts can be applied to any business, including bootstrapped startups. These principles emphasize reducing waste, increasing value, and constantly improving processes to improve efficiency and effectiveness.

The following are the key principles of lean operations:

- **Value identification:** Determine what your customers value in your product or service and focus on delivering that value while minimizing non-value-added activities.

- *Analyze the entire process of delivering your product* or service, from idea generation to delivery, and identify areas of waste and inefficiencies.

- **Creating a continuous flow:** Streamline your processes and remove bottlenecks to ensure that each step in the process is completed efficiently and without delays.

- *Implementing a pull system entails transitioning* from a push system in which work is pushed onto the next step regardless of its capacity to a pull system in which work is pulled only when the next step is ready to receive it.

- **Pursuing perfection:** Strive for continuous improvement by identifying and eliminating waste, increasing efficiency, and improving the value delivered to customers.

Implementing lean principles in your bootstrapped startup can result in significant gains in efficiency, effectiveness, and customer satisfaction. You can optimize your operations and better allocate resources to the areas that contribute the most to the growth and success of your startup by minimizing waste, maximizing value, and continuously seeking opportunities for process improvement. To summarize, understanding and implementing lean principles is vital for any entrepreneur looking to optimize their operations and maximize the potential of their startup.

Streamlining Business Processes

You can reduce costs, increase productivity, and ultimately improve the overall performance of your business by identifying and eliminating bottlenecks, redundancies, and inefficiencies.

Begin by mapping out your current processes and analyzing each step to see where you can improve. Look for bottlenecks, or points in the process where work is slowed or stopped, and redundancies, which occur when the same task is performed multiple times or by different team members. Analyze the overall efficiency of each process to see if any unnecessary steps or resources are being used.

Once you've identified areas for improvement, consider

implementing the following strategies to improve the
efficiency of your business processes:

- **Automation:** Use technology and tools to automate
  repetitive tasks, allowing your team to focus on
  higher-value activities.

- *Establish standardized procedures and workflows*
  to ensure consistency in quality and efficiency.

- **Continuous improvement:** Encourage your team to
  identify and implement process improvements on
  an ongoing basis to foster a culture of continuous
  improvement.

- **Cross-training:** Teach members of a team to
  perform multiple tasks or roles, allowing for greater
  flexibility and collaboration.

- *Consider outsourcing non-core tasks* to external
  partners to free up your team's time to focus on
  your startup's core competencies.

You can optimize your operations and ensure your business's long-term competitiveness by identifying and eliminating bottlenecks, redundancies, and inefficiencies. Implementing strategies like automation, standardization, continuous improvement, cross-training, and outsourcing will improve the efficiency of your processes and contribute to your startup's overall success.

Embracing Automation

Automation is an integral part of running a lean bootstrapped startup. You can save valuable time and resources by automating repetitive tasks and workflows, allowing you to focus on more strategic aspects of your business. Automation tools and technology have become more affordable and accessible, making it easier for startups to incorporate them into their day-to-day operations.

Automation can be used to manage finances, invoicing, marketing, sales, customer service, and project management, among other things. Accounting software, for example, can be used to automate financial reporting, invoicing, and expense tracking. Marketing automation platforms, on the other hand, can be used to schedule and manage email campaigns, social media posts, and other marketing activities. Customer relationship management (CRM) systems can help you manage leads and customer interactions more effectively by streamlining sales processes.

Consider your startup's needs as well as the potential return on investment when selecting automation tools (ROI). Invest in scalable solutions that can scale with your company and adapt to changes in processes and workflows.

Embracing automation is a powerful way to optimize the operations of your bootstrapped startup, save time, and cut costs. You can improve efficiency and productivity while allowing your team to focus on higher-value activities that drive growth and success by identifying tasks and workflows that can be automated and selecting the right tools.

Implementing Agile Project Management

Agile project management places a premium on flexibility, adaptation, and iterative improvements, making it a suitable method for startups navigating a volatile and uncertain business landscape.

Agile approaches enable bootstrapped firms to respond to changes in market conditions or client demand more efficiently. Working in short, targeted sprints and reviewing progress on a regular basis allows your team to swiftly discover areas for growth and adapt strategy accordingly. This iterative method assures that your startup is continually progressing, even when confronted with unanticipated challenges.

Furthermore, agile project management promotes team collaboration and communication. Your team can operate more efficiently, spot possible difficulties earlier, and make better decisions if you develop an open communication and shared accountability culture. This collaborative approach can help you save time and money while also contributing to the overall success of your bootstrapped firm.

By emphasizing flexibility, adaptation, and incremental improvements, agile project management approaches can considerably assist your bootstrapped firm. This method allows your team to respond to changes more effectively, operate more efficiently, and constantly update your product or service offering to better fit with market needs and wants. You may streamline your operations and processes by implementing agile project management, assuring the long-term survival and growth of your bootstrapped organization.

Building a Culture of Continuous Improvement

Developing a culture of continuous improvement within your bootstrapped startup is essential for remaining competitive and encouraging innovation. You can empower your team to identify opportunities for improvement and drive positive change by encouraging experimentation, ongoing learning, and a growth mindset.

Setting the tone from the top is one way to foster a culture of continuous improvement. Your attitude toward growth, learning, and adaptability as the founder will set an example for your team. Show your dedication to continuous improvement by being open to feedback, reviewing processes on a regular basis, and embracing new ideas and technologies.

Encourage your team members to share their thoughts and suggestions for improvement, and foster an open and collaborative environment in which they can do so. Allow for regular brainstorming sessions and workshops where everyone can contribute and learn from one another.

Invest in your team's professional development by providing training and resources to help them grow. In-house workshops, online courses, and even attending industry conferences are examples of this. By providing learning opportunities, you demonstrate your commitment to their personal and professional development, and they will be more motivated to contribute to your company's continuous improvement.

Implementing a system for tracking and measuring progress toward improvement goals is another effective strategy. Setting clear objectives and tracking progress allows you to identify areas for improvement while also celebrating successes along the way.

By leading by example, encouraging collaboration, investing in the development of your team, and tracking progress, you can foster an environment in which innovation and improvement are actively pursued, resulting in a more efficient and competitive business.

Prioritizing Tasks and Projects

In this section, we'll discuss how to prioritize activities and projects based on their potential effect and alignment with the aims and objectives of your company.

To begin, it's key to have a firm grasp of your startup's goals and objectives, since these will serve as the foundation for your prioritizing efforts. Once your goals and objectives have been established, analyze activities and projects in terms of their potential impact on meeting these targets, as well as the resources needed to complete them.

The Eisenhower Matrix is a valuable technique for prioritizing activities and projects since it categorizes tasks based on their urgency and relevance. Urgent and important tasks should be prioritized and addressed right away, whereas less urgent but still important work can be planned for later. Activities that are neither urgent nor vital should be assigned or, if possible, removed.

The MoSCoW method, which involves categorizing tasks as Must have, Should have, Could have, or Won't have, is another way to task and project prioritization. This strategy allows you to prioritize the most important chores first, ensuring that they are done before moving on to less important ones.

Consider the Pareto Principle (also known as the 80/20 rule), which claims that 80% of the time, 80% of the effort produces 80% of the results. You may maximize your startup's efficiency and progress toward its goals by identifying and focusing on the most important tasks and initiatives.

To summarize, task and project prioritization is a major element of lean operations and process optimization for bootstrapped firms. You can effectively allocate your limited resources to the most influential efforts by using strategies such as the Eisenhower Matrix, MoSCoW approach, and Pareto Principle, allowing your startup to fulfill its goals and objectives more efficiently.

Managing Remote Teams

As more firms adopt remote work arrangements, mastering the skill of managing remote teams becomes increasingly vital for bootstrapped entrepreneurs. You can assure successful communication, collaboration, and productivity in a dispersed work environment by following these best practices.

- **Provide clear communication channels:** Use systems like Slack, Microsoft Teams, or Google Chat to help team members communicate more effectively. Establish expectations for responsiveness and make sure everyone knows which channels to use for different sorts of communication.

- *Conduct regular virtual meetings*, such as weekly or bi-weekly team meetings, to maintain a sense of connection and to enable open discussions. To improve cooperation, encourage active participation and employ screen-sharing tools.

- **Establish clear objectives and goals:** Ensure that each team member understands their roles, deadlines, and performance expectations. Set SMART goals and monitor progress on a regular basis to ensure alignment and accountability.

- *Encourage a culture of trust and autonomy* by allowing your remote team members to control their own workloads and schedules. Promote autonomy and offer assistance when needed, but avoid micromanagement.

- **Use project management tools:** Track tasks, deadlines, and progress using tools like Trello, Asana, or Basecamp. These technologies can aid in the organization and accountability of team members while also offering visibility into the overall state of projects.

- **Promote virtual team-building activities:** To foster camaraderie and strengthen relationships among distant team members, organize virtual social events like as online game evenings, happy hours, or coffee breaks.

- **Provide continuing training and development opportunities:** Provide your remote team members access to online courses, webinars, or workshops to enable them continue to enhance their abilities and keep current on industry trends.

Effective remote team management necessitates clear communication, regular virtual meetings, goal setting, trust, project management tools, team-building activities, and continual training opportunities. By employing these best practices, you can ensure that your remote workforce remains engaged, productive, and connected, thus assisting your bootstrapped startup's success.

Establishing Standard Operating Procedures (SOPs)

As a bootstrapped startup, consistency and efficiency in all parts of your business are fundamental. Standard Operating Procedures (SOPs) are critical in accomplishing this. This part will go through the importance of developing and executing SOPs in your startup, as well as the benefits they give.

SOPs are recorded, step-by-step guidelines that define how specific tasks inside your startup should be completed. They aid in the development of a consistent and standardized method to carrying out numerous activities, which can lead to enhanced productivity, fewer errors, and higher work quality. Furthermore, SOPs serve as a foundation for training new team members as well as a reference point for existing employees, ensuring that everyone is on the same page when it comes to task execution.

It is necessary to involve your team members in the process of developing effective SOPs. Get feedback from people who are directly involved in the tasks being documented, and ensure that the SOPs are clear, short, and simple to follow. Review and update your SOPs on a regular basis to reflect changes in procedures, technology, or business objectives.

SOPs can help to reduce risks associated with employee turnover or knowledge gaps within the business, in addition to boosting efficiency and consistency. You can ensure that essential information and processes are retained by implementing consistent procedures, even if team members come and depart.

Adopting Standard Operating Procedures is a core part of running a successful bootstrapped firm. SOPs help to maintain consistency and efficiency in all elements of your business, resulting in better productivity, fewer errors, and higher work quality. You may develop a culture of continuous improvement and optimize your operations for long-term success by involving your team members in the creation and execution of SOPs.

Monitoring and Measuring Performance

By developing and monitoring key performance indicators (KPIs) for your startup, you can guarantee that your plans are producing the required outcomes and make data-driven decisions to improve your operations.

To begin, it is important to decide on the key performance indicators (KPIs) that are most relevant to the objectives and operational goals of your bootstrapped firm. Revenue growth, client acquisition cost, customer lifetime value, conversion rates, and operational efficiency measures are all common

KPIs to evaluate. Once you've chosen the right KPIs for your company, set up a system for tracking and reporting on these indicators on a regular basis.

Use tools and technologies, including as dashboards and data visualization platforms, to make tracking and analyzing your KPIs easier. By continuously monitoring the performance of your startup, you can immediately find areas for development, change your tactics, and optimize your operations for optimum efficiency and growth.

For bootstrapped startups looking to optimize their operations and procedures, monitoring and measuring performance through meaningful KPIs is necessary. Tracking these indicators on a regular basis allows you to evaluate the performance of your tactics and make data-driven decisions for ongoing improvement. Adopting this method will ultimately add to your bootstrapped startup's long-term success and sustainability.

Let's move on to Chapter 11: Mastering Sales & Customer Acquisition, where we'll look at methods and tactics for successfully gaining customers and driving revenue development in your bootstrapped firm.

11

MASTERING SALES & CUSTOMER ACQUISITION

~

"Please send me more leads!" is a popular request in the lead generation industry. The key to success, however, is not merely accumulating more leads, but also properly nurturing and exploiting the prospects you already have.

I started working in sales when I was 17, selling cars over the summer. My manager was frequently irritated with me for failing to follow up with potential customers. I decided to follow up with a couple who had expressed interest in a car, and they ended up purchasing it. They thanked me for calling, and I learned a valuable lesson that day.

As my career grew and I began working with clients in a recurring revenue model, I realized that the best customers are the ones who return. This showed me the importance of staying in touch with clients and achieving high levels of satisfaction.

My experience emphasized the significance of having a well-structured sales system in place, complete with a defined strategy, pipeline, communication plan, and data-driven processes to provide your team with the resources they need to maximize revenue potential with each opportunity.

In this chapter, we'll look at the key components of a good sales and customer acquisition plan and how to put them into action in your bootstrapped startup to achieve long-term growth.

Understanding Your Target Audience

Understanding your target audience is the cornerstone of any effective sales and customer acquisition plan. With a thorough grasp of your clients' goals, desires, and pain spots, you can personalize your product or service offering to meet their individual needs. This not only increases the likelihood of a sale, but it also develops consumer loyalty and repeat business.

It is important to undertake market research and collect data on your target audience's demographics, interests, and behavior patterns in order to successfully comprehend them. This data can then be utilized to develop specific customer personas that represent your ideal clients. These personas can help you steer your sales and marketing efforts by crafting targeted messages and offers that resonate with your target audience.

Furthermore, understanding your target audience's pain areas will assist you in positioning your product or service as the solution to their difficulties. By displaying empathy and a genuine desire to assist your consumers, you will be able to establish trust and credibility, all of which are necessary for effective sales and customer acquisition.

Recognizing your target demographic is key for successfully selling your product or service and expanding your customer base. You'll be more positioned to engage with your customers and meet their demands if you undertake rigorous market research, create detailed client personas, and address their pain areas. This will lay the groundwork for a successful sales and customer acquisition plan.

Crafting a Compelling Value Proposition

A well-crafted value proposition is necessary for your boot-strapped startup's success. It communicates to your target audience the unique benefits of your product or service and distinguishes you from competition.

Here's how to craft a compelling value proposition that will appeal to your target market:

- **Identify the distinct advantages of your product or service:** Determine the essential characteristics and benefits of your offering that set it apart from the competition. Concentrate on what distinguishes and adds value to your product or service for your target audience.

- **Address the pain issues of your target audience:** Explain how your product or service solves the challenges that your target audience is experiencing. Utilize language that appeals to them and indicates your comprehension of their requirements.

- **Be clear and concise:** Your value proposition should be simple to grasp and should capture the essence of your service in a few phrases. Jargon and buzzwords should be avoided because they might cause misunderstanding and obfuscate your message.

- *Customer feedback, market research, and A/B
  testing may all be used* to test and develop your
  value offer over time. Iterate and refine your
  messaging on a regular basis to ensure that it
  remains relevant and interesting to your target
  audience.

Throughout the sales and customer acquisition process, a compelling value proposition is key for attracting and converting potential clients. You can establish a value proposition that resonates with your customers and drives growth for your bootstrapped firm by identifying your target demographic, emphasizing your unique benefits, solving pain spots, and refining your message.

Developing a Sales Funnel

In today's competitive marketplace, having an effective sales funnel in place to nurture leads and convert them into customers is essential for bootstrapped startups. A well-designed sales funnel can help you optimize your customer acquisition process and increase revenue.

A sales funnel is based on the assumption that prospects move through a number of phases before making a purchase decision. Awareness, interest, contemplation, conversion, and retention are common stages. The sales funnel allows you to visualize and understand your potential customers' journey, allowing you to develop customized marketing and sales strategies that address their individual demands and pain points at each stage.

Here are some guidelines to help you create and optimize a sales funnel for your bootstrapped startup:

- **Raise awareness:** Raise awareness of your product or service through numerous marketing channels such as social media, content marketing, public relations, and advertising.

- **Generate leads:** Attract new clients by providing helpful content in exchange for their contact information, such as blog entries, whitepapers, or webinars. This can assist you in compiling a list of prospects who have expressed an interest in your product or service.

- *Lead nurturing entails engaging with leads* via individualized email marketing campaigns, social media interactions, and focused content that meets their specific requirements and pain areas.

- **Turn leads into customers:** As prospects progress through the funnel, employ focused sales approaches to encourage them to buy, such as product demos, free trials, or special specials.

- **Keep consumers and encourage repeat business:** Following a successful sale, continue to interact with your customers by giving excellent customer service, soliciting feedback, and delivering relevant material or promotions to keep them coming back for more.

- **Evaluate and improve your funnel:** Review the success of your sales funnel on a regular basis, find areas for improvement, and optimize your strategy to increase conversions and revenue.

You can design focused marketing and sales campaigns

that effectively take prospects from awareness to conversion, eventually producing growth and revenue for your organization, by understanding and optimizing each stage of the funnel.

Leveraging Sales Tools and Software

Bootstrapped firms must leverage existing resources and technology to optimize sales processes and boost customer acquisition in today's highly competitive business environment. Startups can improve their sales efforts, increase productivity, and gain a competitive advantage by employing sales tools and software such as CRMs, proposal tools, phone systems, and integrated lead sources.

This section will go through how to use these tools to drive client acquisition and growth.

- **CRM Systems:** Customer Relationship Management (CRM) systems are critical tools for managing customer contacts and tracking leads as they go through the sales funnel. CRMs can help you optimize your sales efforts and boost conversion rates by organizing customer information, automating sales processes, and offering important insights into customer behavior. Pick a CRM that meets your needs and suits your budget, and make sure it integrates with other sales tools for seamless data flow.

- **Proposal Tools:** Without the correct tools, creating and managing sales proposals may be time-consuming and error-prone. Proposal software allows you to quickly and easily build professional, personalized proposals. These tools assist you in streamlining the proposal process, tracking client interactions, and closing agreements more quickly. For best efficiency, look for proposal solutions that interact with your CRM and other sales tools.

- **Phone Systems:** Managing customer communications and ensuring a seamless sales process requires a dependable and feature-rich phone system. To keep your sales staff connected and informed, modern phone systems provide capabilities such as call routing, voicemail-to-email, and call analytics. To increase your team's efficiency and improve customer interactions, use a phone system that connects with your CRM and other sales tools.

- **Integrated Lead Sources:** Lead generation and management are critical components of any sales process. You can assure a consistent flow of qualified leads into your sales funnel by integrating lead sources such as social media, email marketing, and content marketing into your sales tools. To maximize your marketing and sales activities, measure and analyze the performance of multiple lead sources.

You may improve productivity, promote growth, and get a competitive edge in the market by combining CRM systems, proposal tools, phone systems, and integrated lead sources into your sales strategy. Investing in the proper tools and technology can have a big impact on the success of your firm and help you reach your business goals.

Building Relationships and Trust

Fostering authentic connections with potential clients is more important than ever in today's competitive business world, as it can result in long-term consumer loyalty and positive word-of-mouth.

In this section, we'll go over the importance of delivering value, providing outstanding service, and exhibiting knowledge to build long-term relationships with your clients.

- **Providing Value:** Focus on providing value from the start if you want to create solid relationships with your potential customers. Analyze their problems and provide answers that truly meet their needs. You may pique their curiosity and present your startup as an useful partner in their success by giving helpful material, insights, or tools.

- **Superb Customer Service:** Customer service can make or break a business, especially for bootstrapped businesses that rely on customer satisfaction and referrals. Try to outperform your customers' expectations by providing prompt, personalized, and efficient service. Customers who feel valued and well-served are more likely to become devoted supporters of your company and refer you to others.

- *Building trust with potential customers requires demonstrating your competence in your industry* or area. Offer your expertise, experience, and one-of-a-kind insights through multiple platforms such as blog entries, webinars, and social media updates. You can position your bootstrapped firm as an authority in your sector by showing your expertise, making it easier for potential buyers to trust your products or services.

You can develop true connections that lead to long-term client loyalty and success for your organization by continually offering value, providing outstanding service, and exhibiting knowledge. Keeping these concepts in mind will not only help you acquire new consumers, but will also turn them into brand ambassadors, assuring a continual stream of referrals and new prospects.

Sales Techniques and Strategies

Even with little resources, smart sales approaches and strategies can help you acquire new clients and produce income.

We'll look at some notable sales approaches and strategies that can help your bootstrapped startup, such as consultative selling, solution selling, and inbound sales, in this section.

- *Consultative Selling is a sales strategy that focuses on knowing the customer's needs*, issues, and goals. You may create rapport and trust with your prospects by asking open-ended questions and actively listening, positioning yourself as a competent advisor rather than just a salesperson. This method enables you to provide customized solutions that truly address your clients' needs, perhaps leading to improved conversion rates and customer satisfaction.

- **Solution Selling:** A sales process that stresses identifying and addressing the customer's pain areas through your product or service is known as solution selling. You may explain how your service can address their problems and enhance their condition by emphasizing on the value that your solution delivers to the customer. This strategy necessitates a thorough grasp of your target market, as well as the ability to successfully express the benefits and advantages of your product or service.

- *Inbound sales is a sales technique that uses content marketing, search engine optimization (SEO), social media, and other digital channels to attract potential consumers*. You may generate leads and convert them into customers by generating quality content and resources that address the requirements and interests of your target audience. This strategy can be especially beneficial for bootstrapped firms because it often involves less initial investment than standard outbound sales approaches like cold phoning or direct mail.

You may engage your target audience, illustrate the value of your product or service, and ultimately drive revenue and growth for your organization by focusing on consultative selling, solution selling, and inbound sales. To find the tactics that work best for your startup and your consumers, you must experiment with multiple ways and constantly enhance your sales process.

Following Up and Nurturing Leads

In this section, we'll look at how timely follow-ups and nurturing leads may help you create trust, stay top of mind, and eventually convert prospects into paying customers.

- *Following up on and nurturing leads* are *major elements of any bootstrapped startup's sales strategy.* Prospects rarely become clients after the initial meeting. It needs frequent and purposeful involvement to keep your startup on their radar and establish trust.

- *Timely follow-ups reflect your dedication* to meeting the demands of the prospect and demonstrate that you value their time and attention. Following up shortly after initial contact allows you to stand out from the crowd and keep your prospect's attention.

- *Lead nurturing is a continuing process* that entails sending important information, updates, and insights to your prospects on a frequent basis. You may create trust and credibility with your target audience by posting useful content and engaging in meaningful dialogues. This strategy keeps you at the front of prospects' minds and raises the possibility that they will choose your startup when they are ready to make a purchase decision.

- Consider using a *Customer Relationship Management (CRM) system to track* interactions, plan follow-ups, and analyze the performance of your engagement techniques to maximize your lead nurturing efforts. Personalizing your messages and utilizing different channels, including as email, phone calls, and social media, can also help to improve your lead nurturing efforts.

Following up on prospects and nurturing them are significant phases in the sales and client acquisition process. You boost the likelihood of turning prospects into paying customers and fueling the growth of your bootstrapped firm by continuously engaging with them, delivering value, and creating trust.

Tracking and Measuring Sales Performance

When it comes to managing sales and customer acquisition in a bootstrapped startup, the necessity of setting sales targets, tracking key performance indicators (KPIs), and analyzing data cannot be emphasized.

These techniques will enable you to optimize your sales strategies, produce greater results, and ensure the long-term viability of your company.

- **Establishing Sales Goals:** Well defined sales goals provide direction and purpose for your sales staff, pushing them to work toward measurable targets. These objectives should be specific, measurable, attainable, relevant, and time-bound (SMART) in order to be realistic and effective in guiding your sales efforts.

- **Tracking Key Performance Indicators (KPIs):** KPIs are critical for tracking your sales team's progress and the effectiveness of your sales initiatives. The amount of leads generated, conversion rates, average transaction size, and customer acquisition costs are all common sales KPIs. By measuring these indicators on a regular basis, you may identify areas for improvement and adapt your plans accordingly.

- **Data Analysis:** Gathering and evaluating data about your sales success allows you to make more educated decisions and optimize your sales procedures. Customer demographics, purchasing habits, and market developments should all be included in this analysis. You may better target your sales efforts and obtain greater outcomes by gaining insights from this data.

For bootstrapped firms, tracking and assessing sales success are steps in mastering sales and customer acquisition. You may modify your sales methods, enhance your performance, and eventually expand your organization by defining SMART goals, monitoring KPIs, and evaluating data.

Creating a Customer-Centric Culture

You can build an environment that supports repeat business, drives referrals, and differentiates you from the competition by prioritizing customer happiness and ensuring that your entire staff is aligned with this aim.

The following are some essential tactics for developing a customer-centric culture:

- **Establish your customer service values:** Begin by outlining the essential ideals that will guide your company's customer service strategy. These ideals should be clear, actionable, and effectively communicated to all team members.

- **Hire for cultural fit:** Prioritize applicants that share your company's customer service values and have a track record of creating outstanding customer experiences when hiring new team members.

- **Train and empower your staff:** Invest in extensive training programs that will provide your team with the skills and knowledge required to provide great customer service. Let them to make decisions that benefit the consumer, even if it means occasionally breaking business standards.

- **Measure and reward performance:** Create key performance indicators (KPIs) for client satisfaction and use them to track the success of your team. Employees that consistently provide exceptional customer service and contribute to a customer-centric culture should be recognized and rewarded.

- *Promote open communication and collaboration* among members of your team. This will not only aid in the identification of areas for improvement, but it will also guarantee that best practices are communicated and embraced throughout the firm.

- *Solicit consumer input on a regular basis* to uncover areas for development and gain insights into their preferences and problem concerns. Utilize this data to help shape your company's strategy and drive continual improvement.

- **Iterate and improve:** Evaluate your company's customer service performance on a regular basis, making modifications and enhancements as appropriate. This dedication to continuous development will help to ensure that your organization remains responsive to your consumers' evolving demands and expectations.

You can drive repeat business, generate referrals, and set

your startup on a path to sustainable success by prioritizing customer satisfaction and employing techniques that promote a customer-focused mindset.

Customer Retention and Upselling

Not only is it less expensive to keep customers than to recruit new ones, but happy consumers are more likely to refer others to your company and help it grow.

This section will go through ideas for increasing revenue through client retention and upselling.

- **Emphasize customer service:** Excellent client service is essential for customer retention and loyalty. Make sure your team is responsive, helpful, and empathic when it comes to handling client wants and issues.

- *Make your consumers feel appreciated* by personalizing their experiences to their tastes and needs. Create personalized offers, communications, and suggestions using data and insights gleaned from customer interactions.

- *Encourage clients to provide feedback* on their experiences with your products or services on a regular basis, and utilize this knowledge to improve and adjust your offers.

- **Provide loyalty programs or incentives:** To encourage repeat business, reward long-term consumers with loyalty programs or incentives like as discounts or exclusive access to new items or services.

- **Find chances for upselling and cross-selling:**
  Examine your consumers' wants and look for ways
  to offer them extra products or services that match
  their present purchases. This has the potential to
  boost income and customer pleasure.

- **Keep in touch:** Get in touch with your consumers
  on a frequent basis via newsletters, social media, or
  personalized outreach to keep them up to date on
  new products, services, or promotions.

- **Improve your products and services on a regular
  basis:** Review your offers on a regular basis and
  make modifications based on client feedback,
  industry trends, and your own observations to
  ensure that you're always providing the greatest
  available solutions for your consumers.

You can create enduring relationships with your
customers and a strong foundation for your business by
prioritizing customer service, personalizing experiences, and
proactively recognizing chances for upselling or cross-selling.

Let's go on to Chapter 12: Overcoming Challenges and
Staying Resilient.

12

OVERCOMING CHALLENGES AND STAYING RESILIENT

❧

My entrepreneurial experience has been riddled with ups and downs. There were occasions when I was totally exhausted when I left the office, like the time I waited for a train that never showed and had to call an Uber while feeling on the point of a mental breakdown. There were moments of anxiety and panic, such as when our biggest client let us go at the start of the COVID-19 pandemic, or when a dissatisfied client threatened legal action.

Despite these hurdles, I also had tremendous victories. I always made payroll on time, and I was rewarded with substantial customer victories. Our team celebrated our accomplishments collectively, such as the business trip to Cabo after achieving our revenue targets.

Along this journey, I've discovered that resilience is the key to entrepreneurship success. In this chapter, we'll look at tactics for overcoming obstacles and remaining resilient in the face of hardship.

Identifying Common Startup Challenges

Due to their limited resources and reliance on self-funding, bootstrapped businesses frequently confront a unique set of obstacles.

In this section, we'll go through some of the most frequent issues that bootstrapped firms confront, such as limited resources, financial demands, and preserving work-life balance. Knowing these hurdles can help you prepare for them and remain resilient as you pursue achievement.

- *Bootstrapped firms often have fewer financial resources* at their disposal than those with external capital. This can lead to employment, marketing, and product development limits, making it critical to be resourceful and inventive in finding ways to grow your firm with limited resources.

- **Financial Pressures:** For bootstrapped entrepreneurs, a lack of external investment can result in considerable financial demands. It is possible that you will find yourself juggling personal and professional financial obligations, which can be stressful and difficult. To negotiate these demands, it is critical to establish solid financial management skills and maintain a disciplined approach to budgeting.

- **Preserving Work-Life Balance:** To keep their firms afloat, bootstrapped entrepreneurs frequently work long hours and wear numerous hats. This can make maintaining a healthy work-life balance challenging and may lead to burnout. Set limits, prioritize self-care, and delegate responsibilities where possible to avoid this.

Bootstrapped startups have a particular set of obstacles, such as limited resources, financial constraints, and achieving work-life balance. By being aware of these obstacles, you can devise tactics to overcome them and remain resilient as you grow your firm. To ensure the long-term success and sustainability of your bootstrapped firm, embrace resourcefulness and ingenuity, acquire solid financial management skills, and prioritize work-life balance.

Embracing Failure as a Learning Opportunity

Failure is an unavoidable component of the entrepreneurial path. Failures and setbacks, on the other hand, must be approached with the appropriate perspective, viewing them as useful learning experiences that can provide insights and guidance for future initiatives.

In this section, we'll discuss the importance of viewing failure as a learning opportunity and offer suggestions for adopting this perspective.

- **The Importance of Accepting Failure:** Seeing failures and setbacks as chances for growth can help you develop resilience, perseverance, and a growth mentality. You can get useful insights into future decisions and prevent making the same mistakes by assessing what went wrong and identifying opportunities for improvement. This approach can lead to a more resilient company that is better prepared for the inevitable problems that lie ahead.

Adoption of a Learning Mindset Recommendations:

- **Reflect on your experiences:** After a failure or setback, take the time to think about what you can learn from it. Consider what went wrong, what you could have done differently, and how you can use these lessons in the future.

- **Request input:** Don't be reluctant to approach your team, mentors, or peers for feedback. Their viewpoints can assist you in identifying areas for improvement and provide crucial insights that you may have missed.

- *See failure as a chance for progress* and be willing to adapt and evolve depending on the lessons you've learned.

- **Exercise self-compassion:** Remember that everyone has setbacks, and it's critical to treat yourself with compassion and understanding during these trying moments.

Seeing failure as a learning opportunity is an important perspective for bootstrapped entrepreneurs. You may develop resilience, make better-informed decisions, and ultimately build a stronger, more flexible startup by viewing setbacks as opportunities for development and learning. As you traverse the entrepreneurial journey, remember to reflect on your experiences, seek criticism, be open to change, and practice self-compassion.

Building a Strong Support Network

A network of mentors, peers, and trusted advisers may provide invaluable counsel, encouragement, and support during trying times.

In this section, we'll discuss how to develop a strong support network for the achievement of your startup.

- **The Value of a Support Network:** A strong support network can provide emotional support, counsel, and connections that can assist you in overcoming difficulties, making better decisions, and accessing new opportunities. Surrounding yourself with people who understand the unique challenges of entrepreneurship can reduce stress, boost motivation, and help you grow personally and professionally.

  Strategies for Creating a Support Network:

- *Engage in industry conferences,* meetings, and other networking events to interact with other entrepreneurs and professionals who may offer support and guidance.

- **Participate in online communities:** Participate in online forums, social media groups, and platforms such as LinkedIn to locate peers who share your interests and can offer useful insights and guidance.

- **Look for mentors:** Determine seasoned entrepreneurs or industry experts who can provide tailored advice and help based on their own experiences and knowledge.

- **Make use of your existing connections:** To broaden your support network and create relationships with people who can offer encouragement and advise, reach out to friends, family, past colleagues, or alumni networks.

- **Be willing to collaborate:** Work with other entrepreneurs or industry professionals to share experiences, learn from one another, and build mutually beneficial partnerships.

- **Keeping and Growing Your Support Network:** Creating a solid support network is a continuous activity. Maintain and nurture relationships by staying in touch, offering assistance when required, and actively participating in conversations and events.

By following the advice provided above and devoting time and effort to developing and maintaining relationships, you will develop a network of mentors, peers, and trusted advisers who can provide insight, encouragement, and support through difficult times. This support system will assist you in remaining resilient and maintaining your momentum on the road to success.

Practicing Effective Time Management

Effective time management is essential for bootstrapped entrepreneurs, who frequently wear multiple hats and juggle multiple obligations. Remaining focused and productive in the face of hurdles and disappointments is an important success ability.

In this section, we'll discuss time management and task

prioritization tactics to help you overcome obstacles and remain resilient.

- **The Significance of Time Management:** Good time management allows you to work smarter, not harder, by increasing productivity and allocating your time and energy to the most important activities. This allows you to stay on track with your objectives, establish a healthy work-life balance, and deal with setbacks more effectively.

The following time management tactics can help you manage your time more effectively:

- **Establish clear priorities:** Determine the tasks that are most important to the success of your company and focus on accomplishing them first. This will assist you in being focused and making the greatest use of your time.

- **Tasks should be broken down into manageable chunks:** Breaking down major activities into smaller, more achievable steps might help you retain momentum and feel less overwhelmed.

- **Make use of time-blocking:** To be focused and productive, assign certain time blocks to different jobs or activities and limit distractions during these times.

- **Outsource and delegate:** Determine which jobs can be assigned or outsourced to free up time for high-priority activities.

- **Review and adjust on a regular basis:** Review your calendar and priorities on a regular basis to ensure that you're spending your time wisely and making adjustments as needed.

Remember to evaluate your time management methods on a regular basis and make changes as needed to ensure that you're using your time wisely and keeping on track for success.

Managing Stress and Avoiding Burnout

As a bootstrapped business founder, you will almost certainly confront multiple hurdles and high-pressure scenarios. To avoid burnout, preserve mental and emotional well-being, and remain resilient, it is essential to detect and handle stress.

In this section, we'll talk about the importance of stress management and offer advice on how to strike a healthy work-life balance.

- **The Significance of Stress Management:**
  Prolonged stress can have serious effects for your mental and physical health, reducing your productivity and decision-making abilities. You may avoid burnout and preserve the resilience required to manage the ups and downs of entrepreneurship by recognizing and managing stress.

- **Stress Management and Burnout Prevention:**
  Consider applying the following ways to maintain your mental and emotional well-being:

- *Create clear boundaries* between your professional and personal life, making sure to schedule time for relaxation, hobbies, and social relationships.

- Emphasize activities that *enhance physical, emotional, and mental well-being*, such as regular exercise, a balanced diet, and appropriate sleep, when practicing self-care.

- **Get help:** Don't be afraid to seek help from friends, family, or professional support networks to help you manage stress and negotiate difficult situations.

- **Tasks should be broken down into manageable chunks:** Cutting projects down into smaller, more manageable chunks might help them feel less overwhelming and reduce stress.

- *Acknowledge when you need assistance* and delegate chores to your team or outsource specific jobs to lessen your workload and stress.

- **Mindfulness exercises:** To relieve stress and maintain a sense of calm, use mindfulness practices such as meditation or deep breathing exercises.

Controlling stress and preventing burnout are key for preserving the resilience required to succeed in the difficult environment of business. You can safeguard your mental and emotional well-being and be better prepared to tackle challenges and opportunities by setting boundaries, practicing self-care, seeking help, and applying stress-reduction measures. Remember that self-care is an essential component of remaining resilient and achieving long-term success in your bootstrapped firm.

Navigating Uncertainty and Adapting to Change

Uncertainty is a frequent companion in the world of startups, particularly those that are bootstrapped. Adaptability and flexibility in the face of change can mean the difference between success and failure.

In this section, we'll emphasize the need of adaptability and flexibility, as well as provide assistance for making informed judgments and altering techniques as needed.

- **The Importance of Adaptability:** Any entrepreneur must be able to adapt to changing conditions. The business landscape is continuously changing, and your firm must be ready to pivot and modify its tactics in order to remain competitive. Recognizing new opportunities, responding to obstacles, and remaining resilient in the face of adversity are all benefits of adaptation.

- **Making Informed Decisions:** When confronted with ambiguity, it is critical to obtain as much information as possible before making a decision. Keep up to date on industry trends, customer preferences, and competition activity, and utilize this information to influence your decision-making. By making judgments based on reliable evidence, you will enhance your odds of success while decreasing your possibilities of making costly mistakes.

- **Adjusting Strategies:** Be prepared to alter your strategies as needed as you manage the uncertainties that come with running a bootstrapped firm. Review your progress and reassess your goals on a regular basis to ensure they remain relevant to your present situation. Be open to learning from your mistakes and changing your strategy when it becomes clear that a change is required.

You'll be better prepared to meet the obstacles of running a startup if you embrace adaptability, make educated judgments, and modify strategy as needed. Maintaining a growth attitude and remaining resilient can put you in a good position to overcome hurdles and achieve long-term success in your business path.

Celebrating Small Wins

You need to recognize and appreciate tiny triumphs and milestones along the way to developing your startup. These accomplishments, no matter how minor they appear, can play an important role in preserving motivation and momentum, especially when faced with adversity.

In this section, we'll discuss the significance of celebrating modest victories and offer tips on how to do so effectively.

- **The Significance of Identifying and Enjoying Small Wins:** Acknowledging and celebrating tiny triumphs can have a significant impact on the overall success of your startup. These achievements can raise morale, generate a sense of success, and aid in the retention of motivation during difficult times. Furthermore, celebrating little victories can help you and your team create a development mentality by teaching you to appreciate the small steps that contribute to long-term success.

Here are some ideas for recognizing and celebrating little triumphs and milestones in your bootstrapped startup:

- **Celebrate your team's accomplishments:** Make it a practice to share little victories with your team during meetings or through communication channels. This technique not only keeps everyone informed, but it also fosters a culture of appreciation and celebration.

- **Make a graphic depiction of the following:** Create a visual depiction of your startup's development, such as a milestone chart or a progress board, to remind you of your accomplishments.

- **Personal and team incentives:** Provide tiny incentives or awards for completing certain milestones or goals. They can be as simple as a team lunch, additional vacation time, or a little bonus.

- **Regularly evaluate your progress:** Make time at meetings or at the end of the week to reflect on progress and recognize accomplishments and obstacles overcome.

By recognizing and celebrating these accomplishments, you will create a positive environment that promotes resilience and tenacity. Accept the habit of acknowledging little triumphs and watch how it helps to your startup's long-term success and growth.

Maintaining a Long-Term Vision

In the world of bootstrapped startups, it's not uncommon to encounter various obstacles and setbacks on the journey to success. However, maintaining a long-term vision and keeping your eyes on the ultimate goals can help you stay resilient and persevere through these challenges.

In this section, we'll discuss the significance of keeping your long-term goals in mind and offer strategies to help you stay focused and motivated.

- **The Significance of a Long-Term Vision:** Having a clear long-term vision is essential for bootstrapped entrepreneurs because it serves as a guiding force, providing direction and purpose even during difficult times. Your vision should encompass the values, objectives, and aspirations that drive your startup, and it should be ambitious yet achievable. By maintaining a long-term perspective, you'll be better equipped to navigate challenges, stay motivated, and make strategic decisions that align with your ultimate goals.

Keeping your long-term vision at the forefront of your mind can be challenging, especially when faced with immediate obstacles and setbacks. Here are some strategies to help you stay focused and motivated:

- **Regularly revisit your vision:** Make a habit of reviewing your long-term goals and objectives frequently to ensure they remain fresh in your mind.

- **Break down your vision into smaller, manageable goals:** By setting short-term, achievable milestones that align with your long-term vision, you'll be able to maintain momentum and celebrate progress along the way.

- **Surround yourself with supportive individuals:** Engage with mentors, advisors, and peers who share your vision and can offer encouragement, advice, and perspective during challenging times.

- **Stay adaptable:** Be willing to reassess and adjust your vision as needed, based on new information and insights that you gather along your journey.

By keeping your ultimate goals and aspirations in mind, you'll be better prepared to navigate obstacles, make strategic decisions, and remain motivated throughout your startup journey. Embrace the strategies shared here to help you stay focused on your vision and propel your startup toward long-term success.

With the completion of Chapter 12: Overcoming Challenges and Staying Resilient, we'll now move on to Chapter 13: Scaling Your Bootstrapped Startup.

13

SCALING YOUR BOOTSTRAPPED STARTUP

≈

I began to see the rewards of our labor after two years of hard work and dedication. Our services began to gain traction in our niche group, and the relationships and material we had developed began to pay off. It was obvious that we needed to scale our bootstrapped startup.

We had steady recurring revenue, more clients coming to us, an increase in sales calls, over 50 five-star Google reviews, and a more streamlined service offering. Many processes had been automated, making it easier to onboard clients rapidly and retain them for longer periods of time.

When we entered this new stage of growth, I concentrated on optimizing our onboarding processes, upgrading our sales system with a streamlined CRM system and outbound program, investing in customer success, and increasing the customer experience. We even created an app exclusively for field salesmen to help them maximize their leads. Before raising costs, I got access to a line of credit to maintain financial security.

We'll look at the key steps and tactics for growing your

bootstrapped firm, building on the foundation you've already laid, and assuring long-term development and success in this chapter.

Identifying the Right Time to Scale

Understanding when to grow your bootstrapped startup is a key decision that can have far-reaching consequences for your company's success. Waiting too long can result in missed opportunities and stagnation, while scaling too fast might result in financial strain and overextended resources.

This part will go over the indicators that your startup is ready for expansion, such as consistent revenue, a robust customer base, and a well-defined market position.

- *Constant revenue production* is one of the most dependable markers that your firm is ready to scale. If you're experiencing consistent, predictable income and a strong cash flow month after month, it's a sign that your business model is functioning and you can start planning for development.

- *A growing and engaged customer base* is another significant indicator that your firm is ready to scale. Loyal consumers who produce repeat business and refer new clients attest to the value of your product or service and can serve as the foundation for future growth.

- **Well-Defined Market Position:** If your startup has carved out a distinct and well-defined market position, you'll be more likely to succeed while scaling. Your market position should be founded on a distinct value offer, a thorough grasp of your target clients, and the capacity to distinguish yourself from competitors.

- **Robust Operations and Processes:** Before scaling, ensure that your startup's operations and processes are efficient, scalable, and resilient to growth challenges. Internal communication and project management are examples, as are sales and customer support systems.

- **A Skilled, Cohesive Team:** A robust, capable staff is vital for scaling your startup. Your team should be committed to the company's goal, have the necessary skills and knowledge for growth, and be adaptable to new challenges and possibilities.

You can decide when it's time to take the commitment and pursue expansion by regularly monitoring your startup's consistent revenue, strong client base, well-defined market position, robust operations and processes, and competent team. By scaling at the correct time, you may increase your chances of success and ensure your company's long-term viability.

Developing a Scalable Business Model

A scalable business model is critical for any firm, but it is especially important for bootstrapped startups that need to utilize their resources and accomplish growth without relying on outside investment.

In this section, we'll discuss how to create a business strategy that can handle growth without drastically increasing prices or reducing quality.

- *Scalability is important* because it helps your startup to develop and expand its operations without incurring exorbitant expenditures or overburdening your existing infrastructure. You can ensure that your bootstrapped firm remains agile, competitive, and well-positioned to capitalize on new possibilities by establishing a scalable model.

Consider the following elements while developing a scalable business model:

- *Lean operations entail streamlining processes* and eliminating inefficiencies in order to reduce costs and increase production.

- **Automation:** Wherever practical, use automation to eliminate manual labor and increase efficiency.

- *Consider outsourcing non-essential functions* to decrease overhead and allow you to focus on your key strengths.

- *Create standardized processes and systems* that can be simply copied as your company grows.

- *Create pricing methods that are adaptable* to changes in demand and market conditions.

- **Diverse revenue streams:** Develop several streams of income to reduce risks and provide financial stability.

- **Embracing Adaptability:** A scalable business model should be changeable, allowing your startup to pivot or modify its strategy in response to market changes, consumer feedback, and other variables. Review and change your business model on a regular basis to ensure it remains relevant and effective as your startup expands.

You may build a profitable business by focusing on lean operations, automation, outsourcing, standardization, flexible pricing, and diverse income streams.

Implementing Systems and Processes

As your company expands, it becomes increasingly fundamental to build efficient systems and processes that can handle rising workloads while also supporting the smooth operation of your expanding organization.

In this section, we'll discuss the importance of creating systems and processes, as well as how to design them to ensure your startup's continuous success as it grows.

- **The Significance of Systems and Processes:** Putting in place solid systems and processes allows your company to run more efficiently, lowering the risk of errors and allowing your staff to effectively handle a growing workload. You may maintain high levels of customer satisfaction and employee productivity by optimizing operations, which ultimately adds to the continuous success of your startup. Furthermore, by exhibiting a professional and ordered attitude, well-defined systems and processes can help make your organization more appealing to potential investors or acquirers.

When developing systems and processes, it is critical to concentrate on the following key areas:

- *Create defined processes* for lead generation, sales funnel management, and customer onboarding, as well as a system for tracking customer interactions and feedback, in sales and customer management.

- *Establish financial tracking,* planning, and reporting methods to ensure accurate and up-to-date financial data.

- **Human resources and team management:** To attract and retain a competent and motivated team, build mechanisms for hiring, onboarding, performance management, and employee development.

Use software and solutions developed to assist you in managing and automating various elements of your organization. Common alternatives include:

- *Project management software* such as Asana, Trello, or Basecamp are useful for organizing tasks and managing projects.

- *CRM systems,* such as Salesforce or HubSpot, are used to manage sales processes and customer interactions.

- *For financial tracking and reporting,* use QuickBooks or Xero accounting software.

You can provide a solid foundation for growth, maintain high levels of customer satisfaction, and position your startup for long-term success by focusing on important areas and applying tools and strategies. Remember to constantly examine and adjust your systems and processes as you scale to ensure they stay effective and flexible to the changing needs of your growing organization.

Hiring and Developing a Strong Team

A competent, motivated, and cohesive staff is essential for the achievement of any startup, especially one that is boot-strapping.

In this section, we'll discuss how to attract, develop, and retain excellent employees to help your firm expand while preserving a positive company culture.

- **Recruitment Top Talent:** Getting the appropriate people to join your startup starts with a rigorous and targeted recruiting strategy. Create appealing job descriptions that appropriately reflect each position's roles and responsibilities. To reach out to potential prospects, use job boards, social media, and networking events. During interviews, be open about your company's vision, values, and expectations to guarantee alignment with the culture of your startup.

- **Training and Development:** After you've hired the right personnel, devote time and resources to their growth and development. Train and mentor your team members to help them gain new skills and expertise. Encourage them to pursue professional development options that correspond with the goals and objectives of your startup.

- **Keeping Top Talent:** It is just as important to maintain great talent as it is to attract it in the first place. Encourage open communication, cooperation, and invention by creating a good and supportive work atmosphere. To keep your team members motivated and committed to the success of your startup, provide competitive remuneration, perks, and possibilities for growth and advancement.

- **Sustaining a Good Business Culture:** Fostering a sense of belonging and togetherness among your team members requires a strong corporate culture. Create a culture that represents your startup's values, encourages inclusivity and diversity, and stresses work-life balance.

You'll lay a solid basis for your startup's growth and long-term success by focusing on recruiting top personnel, investing in training and development, retaining your best employees, and fostering a healthy company culture. Continue to emphasize these areas as your team grows to ensure that your startup stays an appealing and fulfilling place to work.

Prioritizing Customer Success

You may build a strong brand reputation and a firm platform for growth by assuring customer pleasure, reducing churn, and improving lifetime value.

In this section, we'll talk about how important customer success is when it comes to scaling your firm and give ways for creating excellent customer outcomes.

- **Customer Success' Role:** Customer success is all about assisting your customers in achieving their targeted results with your product or service. Customers who are successful and satisfied are more likely to become loyal, long-term consumers who recommend your company to others. This, in turn, assists you in scaling your firm by recruiting more clients, growing revenue, and developing a solid market reputation.

Consider the following tactics to prioritize customer success in your bootstrapped startup:

- **Onboarding and training:** Offer extensive onboarding and training tools to assist clients in quickly and efficiently getting started with your product or service.

- **Proactive support:** Contact consumers on a frequent basis to offer assistance, collect feedback, and resolve any possible concerns before they escalate.

- **Personalization:** Adapt your interactions with customers to their individual requirements and preferences for a more personalized and meaningful experience.

- **Listening to and responding to feedback:** Invite customers to offer their ideas and opinions, and make an honest effort to incorporate their suggestions into product or service enhancements.

- **Customer satisfaction evaluation:** To assess customer satisfaction and identify areas for improvement, use techniques such as Net Promoter Score (NPS) surveys or customer satisfaction (CSAT) surveys.

By focusing on customer success, you can reduce churn and enhance customer lifetime value by doing the following:

- *Improving your product or service* in response to client feedback and market changes.

- *Preventing churn by identifying at-risk clients* and aggressively addressing their problems.

- *Upselling and cross-selling opportunities* can result in improved revenue and a higher client lifetime value.

- *Developing solid relationships with your clients*, instilling trust, and positioning your startup as a trustworthy partner in their success.

You may create a favorable brand reputation and a strong basis for growth by assuring customer satisfaction, reducing churn, and improving lifetime value. Employing tactics like as full onboarding and training, proactive assistance, personalization, listening to and responding to feedback, and monitoring customer happiness will assist you in achieving customer success and, eventually, scaling your startup.

Expanding Your Product or Service Offerings

When your company achieves traction and your customer base expands, it's necessary to diversify and extend your product or service offerings. This can result in more income,

improved customer happiness, and a more robust organization.

This section will go through how to discover growth
possibilities and successfully launch new products or services .
for your startup.

- **Locating Growth Opportunities:** Begin by
  examining your present customer base and their
  demands to discover the greatest paths for
  increasing your product or service offerings.
  Examine their feedback, demands, and pain points
  for patterns, and explore how you might address
  these concerns with new or improved solutions.
  Keep an eye on market developments and
  competitor offers to spot potential gaps and
  opportunities.

- **Testing New Offerings:** It is critical to evaluate the
  market demand and viability of a new product or
  service before completely committing to it.
  Consider developing a minimum viable product
  (MVP) to test the waters and obtain user feedback.
  This technique reduces risk and guarantees that
  you are investing resources in products or services
  that actually suit the demands of your customers.

- **Marketing and Promotion:** To successfully launch
  a new product or service, a targeted marketing and
  promotion strategy is required. Concentrate on
  articulating the benefits and value of your new
  service to existing consumers while also reaching
  out to new potential customers who might be
  interested in what you have to offer. To spread the
  news about your new product or service, use your

existing marketing channels such as email, social media, and content marketing.

- *Set key performance indicators (KPIs)* to track the success of your new product or service. Sales revenue, client acquisition cost, customer happiness, and market share are examples of such indicators. Monitor these KPIs on a regular basis to evaluate the performance of your new offering and make any necessary adjustments to ensure its success.

- **Scaling and Continuous Improvement:** When your new product or service gains traction, concentrate on increasing its manufacturing, distribution, and support operations to keep up with rising demand. Keep an eye on client feedback and use it to drive ongoing improvement in your products and services. This will assist you in maintaining a competitive advantage and keeping your clients delighted.

You may enhance your revenue streams and better serve your growing client base by recognizing chances for expansion, testing new offerings, effectively marketing and promoting them, measuring their success, and continuously improving them. Remember to remain adaptable and open to input, as this will allow you to make more educated decisions and maintain the long-term success of your increased services.

Scaling Your Marketing Efforts

It's important to scale your marketing activities in order to reach a bigger audience, raise brand awareness, and improve revenue.

In this section, we'll discuss how to effectively scale your marketing methods and adjust them to the changing needs of your startup.

- **Evaluate Your Marketing Data:** Begin by examining the data from your current marketing activities to see what is working well and where there is potential for improvement. To learn more about your audience's activity, preferences, and engagement, use tools like Google Analytics, social media insights, and email marketing analytics.

- **Improve Your Marketing Channels:** Using the information from your study, optimize your marketing channels to focus on the platforms and methods that produce the best results. This could entail fine-tuning your messaging, focusing on certain audience segments, or reallocating your marketing spending to support high-performing channels.

- **Automate Marketing Processes:** As your marketing activities expand, it is key to discover ways to streamline and automate procedures in order to save time and resources. To manage your email marketing, social media scheduling, and lead nurturing operations, consider adopting marketing automation platforms like HubSpot, Mailchimp, or Marketo.

- *As you scale, don't be hesitant to try out new marketing ideas and tactics.* Experiment with alternative content formats, advertising platforms, and targeting options to uncover new growth and engagement potential.

- **Collaboration and networking:** Work with other firms, influencers, or organizations in your field to broaden your reach and raise brand awareness. Collaborative ventures, affiliate marketing, and co-marketing activities can help you reach new audiences and increase the effectiveness of your marketing efforts.

- **Monitor and Adjust:** Always monitor the performance of your marketing strategies and be ready to make changes as needed. Keep up with industry trends and best practices, and be flexible in adapting your marketing efforts to the growth and changing needs of your startup.

You may efficiently grow your reach and create improved sales by analyzing your data, improving your channels, automating operations, testing new methods, and partnering with others. Remember to evaluate and tweak your marketing activities as needed, remaining nimble and adaptive to the changing needs of your firm as it grows.

Strategic Partnerships and Collaborations

Strategic partnerships and collaborations can be a strong method to assist the success of your bootstrapped firm by giving opportunity for improved exposure, resource sharing, and mutual gain.

In this section, we'll go through the advantages of collaborating with complementary businesses or industry influencers, as well as offer tips for forming fruitful collaborations.

Connecting with similar businesses or industry influencers can provide various benefits for your bootstrapped startup, including:

- **Increased visibility and reach:** By cooperating with established businesses or industry influencers, you may tap into their current audience and get higher visibility for your startup.

- **Sharing resources:** Partnerships allow you to share resources such as marketing channels, technology, or knowledge, which can help you save money and speed the growth of your firm.

- **Mutual advantage:** When you collaborate with partners who have complimentary abilities or offerings, both parties profit, resulting in a more durable and effective relationship.

- **Collaboration Suggestions for Success:** Consider the following suggestions for forming effective strategic alliances:

- **Find comparable partners:** Search for complementary products or services, a similar target demographic, or a shared goal and values in your industry.

- **Set clear goals and expectations:** When engaging into a partnership, ensure that all sides have a clear

knowledge of the collaboration's aims and
expectations.

- **Speak openly and on a frequent basis:** Keep open
  channels of communication throughout the
  collaboration, addressing successes, obstacles, and
  any necessary changes.

- **Create a written agreement:** To minimize
  misunderstandings and protect both parties,
  consider drafting a written agreement defining the
  partnership's terms, obligations, and expectations.
  This can help ensure that all parties are on the same
  page and understand their respective roles in the
  collaboration.

- **Constantly analyze and refine the partnership:** As
  your bootstrapped firm grows and evolves, it's
  critical to assess the efficacy of your strategic
  partnerships on a frequent basis and make any
  necessary changes. Setting new goals, revising
  resource-sharing arrangements, or exploring new
  collaboration opportunities may all be part of this.

You can broaden your reach, share resources, and build
mutually beneficial partnerships by collaborating with
complimentary firms or industry influencers. It is critical to
choose the correct partners, establish clear goals and expectations, maintain open communication, and regularly analyze
and refine your collaborations to ensure the success of these
partnerships.

Managing Cash Flow and Financial Sustainability

Maintaining a solid cash flow and guaranteeing financial sustainability become increasingly essential as your bootstrapped firm grows.

This section will provide guidance on managing cash flow, budgeting, forecasting, and acquiring extra funding when needed to support the growth of your firm while reducing financial risks.

- **Budgeting for Growth:** When your company expands, you'll need to evaluate your budget to account for rising spending and revise your financial estimates. Refine your budget on an ongoing basis to ensure that it accurately reflects your startup's current financial status and growth trajectory, and deploy resources effectively to support long-term success.

- **Cash Flow Management:** Maintaining a healthy cash flow is critical to the long-term viability of a bootstrapped startup. Focus on measures such as accelerating receivables collection, negotiating favorable payment terms with suppliers, optimizing inventory levels, and controlling expenses to sustain positive cash flow.

- **Financial Forecasting:** As your firm grows, it is critical to keep your financial predictions up to date. This method will assist you in forecasting future cash flow requirements, identifying potential financial issues, and making data-driven decisions to avoid risks and capitalize on opportunities.

- **Extra Funding:** While bootstrapping is the primary emphasis, your startup may require more capital to support growth. Before obtaining external money, investigate various funding options such as angel investors, venture capital, loans, or grants, and carefully consider the potential impact on your firm.

- **Monitoring Important Metrics:** Keep a watch on key financial measures like sales growth, gross margin, and cash flow to ensure that your firm stays on pace for long-term success. Periodically examining these indicators will assist you in identifying patterns, resolving issues, and making strategic changes to your business model.

You'll be better equipped to negotiate the financial obstacles of expansion if you focus on budgeting, forecasting, and smart resource allocation. Maintain a tight watch on your key financial KPIs and be open to the potential of collecting additional investment if necessary to support your startup's long-term growth.

14

CONCLUSION: THE ROAD TO BOOTSTRAPPED SUCCESS

~

Throughout my entrepreneurial path, I encountered numerous hurdles as well as mistrust and doubt from those around me. People called me broke, told me not to risk it, didn't understand me, and didn't believe in me at first. Yet I put on my blinders and went for my dreams anyway.

As my company grew and succeeded, the same people who had doubted me proceeded to shower me with compliments and praise. As I encountered a bump in the road, however, I heard the very same negative noise. I learned to tune it out once more and keep moving forward.

I want you to know that I believe in you, readers. You can accomplish your objectives and realize your ambitions. "Why not?" and "win the day" are two of my favorite phrases to live by.

"Why not?" reminds me that success is always possible. It represents the mindset that inspires entrepreneurs to push above their limits and chase their dreams, no matter what the odds are.

"Win the day" means taking it one day at a time, climbing the mountain one step at a time, and concentrating on the present moment. By winning day after day, you are accumulating small victories that will lead to long-term success.

Realize that the path to success is filled with obstacles and disappointments. Accept the path, enjoy your accomplishments, and never lose sight of your goals. You can accomplish greatness if you are persistent, determined, and willing to learn and adapt.

Let's look at the main elements to keep in mind as you continue your journey as a bootstrapped entrepreneur.

Reflecting on Your Journey

As we near the end of this guide, it's important to reflect on your experiences as a bootstrapped entrepreneur. While developing a successful startup on a shoestring budget can be difficult, it's important to acknowledge the progress you've made, even if it's been slow and steady.

We'll encourage you to reflect on your journey and celebrate the milestones you've reached along the road in this area.

- *Reflection is important* because it helps you to gauge your progress as a bootstrapped entrepreneur, discover areas where you've succeeded, and appreciate the hurdles you've conquered. This self-evaluation can help you keep perspective and motivation even when things get rough.

- **Milestone Recognition:** Take time to recognize your accomplishments, no matter how minor they may appear. Acknowledging these milestones may strengthen your commitment to your startup and enhance your confidence as an entrepreneur, whether it's getting your first customer, meeting a specific revenue target, or successfully changing your business model.

- **Learning from Setbacks:** Throughout your bootstrapped journey, you will definitely meet setbacks and problems. Instead of concentrating on your issues, concentrate on the lessons you've gained from them and how they've aided your development as an entrepreneur. See these situations as chances for personal and professional growth.

- **Keeping Perspective:** Keep in mind that success as a bootstrapped entrepreneur isn't determined exclusively by rapid growth or immediate profitability. It's about creating a long-term business that reflects your values and goals. Keep this in mind as you continue on your journey, and stay true to your individual route to success.

Accept your development, no matter how slow and steady it is, and stay focused on your vision as you continue down the path to bootstrapped success.

Staying True to Your Values

It's key to recall the values and principles that drove you to start your business in the first place as you move on your path to bootstrapped success.

In this part, we'll remind you of the importance of keeping true to your beliefs and offer some advice on how to do so even as your firm develops and evolves.

- **The Importance of Staying True to Your Values:**
  Your beliefs and ideals serve as the cornerstone of
  your startup and distinguish you from the
  competition. Maintaining your unique identity,
  attracting and retaining loyal consumers, and
  creating a great work environment for your
  employees are all benefits of adhering to these
  values. As your firm grows and evolves, it's critical
  to keep your values at the forefront of your
  decision-making process.

As your company grows, you may confront obstacles that put
your adherence to your principles to the test.

Here are some pointers to help you stick to your principles:

- *Review your startup's mission statement* on a
  regular basis to remind yourself and your team of
  your basic values and purpose.

- **Lead by example:** Your actions as a founder set the
  tone for the entire firm. Be a role model for others
  by demonstrating your dedication to your
  principles in your daily actions and decisions.

- **Encourage a values-driven culture:** Promote open
  communication, recognize and reward people who
  live your beliefs, and give continual training and
  development opportunities that reinforce your
  values.

- **Align your choices with your values:** When
  presented with difficult choices, analyze how each
  alternative corresponds with your values. This
  introspection can assist you in making decisions

that are consistent with your ideals and, as a result, benefit your startup.

You'll be well-equipped to tackle the obstacles and possibilities that lie ahead on the path to bootstrapped success if you examine your mission statement on a frequent basis, lead by example, develop a values-driven culture, and align your decisions with your principles.

Giving Back and Mentoring Others

Giving back to the community and supporting fellow entrepreneurs is a vital facet of the entrepreneurial process, especially for bootstrapped startups. By mentoring others, sharing lessons gained, and building a collaborative culture, you not only help other firms grow and succeed, but you also help the overall ecosystem.

In this section, we'll talk about the importance of giving back and mentoring others, and how it may help your startup as well as the greater entrepreneurial community.

- **The Importance of Giving Back:** Successful bootstrapped businesses frequently have a wealth of information and experience that can be beneficial to those who are just getting started. Sharing your knowledge, experiences, and recommendations can assist others in avoiding frequent traps and accelerating their success. In exchange, knowing that you've made a positive impact on someone else's entrepreneurial journey can give you with a sense of fulfillment and purpose.

- **Mentoring Others:** Acting as a mentor to other entrepreneurs allows you to share your experiences and provide assistance on a variety of business topics, including idea validation, marketing, financial management, and growth strategies. You can contribute to others' success while also learning from their unique perspectives and experiences by assisting them in navigating the hurdles of bootstrapping.

- **Promoting a Collaborative Culture:** Encouraging collaboration among bootstrapped entrepreneurs can result in the flow of ideas, resources, and support. This collaborative environment can drive innovation, make problem resolution easier, and ultimately contribute to the success of all parties involved.

Giving back and mentoring others is an important part of the entrepreneurial journey. You may have a beneficial impact on the wider entrepreneurial community and create the way for continued success in your own startup by sharing your knowledge, assisting fellow entrepreneurs, and building a collaborative culture. Accept the opportunity to help others grow and succeed, as it will only enrich your own path and the greater ecosystem.

Planning for Future Growth

To attain long-term success and stability in your bootstrapped firm, you must build plans and strategies centered on long-term growth.

In this section, we'll provide advice on developing a future plan to ensure that your company is well-positioned to scale and prosper over time.

- **Establishing Growth Objectives:** To begin, set clear, quantifiable growth objectives that correspond with your startup's vision and mission. These objectives should be realistic in terms of your current resources and capabilities, but also ambitious enough to propel your company ahead.

- **Customer-Centric Growth:** Concentrate on strengthening ties with current consumers and constantly enhancing your product or service to meet their changing needs. This customer-centric strategy will not only result in greater revenue from repeat business, but will also assist in the creation of brand champions who may refer new clients to your startup.

- **Diversification and Expansion:** Look for ways to expand your product or service offerings or enter new markets. This can help to reduce risk and strengthen the resilience of your startup in the face of shifting market conditions. Be strategic in your expansion attempts to avoid overextending your resources or diluting your primary strengths.

- **Operational Efficiency:** Review and optimize your startup's processes and systems on a regular basis to ensure that they are scalable and efficient. You may decrease expenses, boost productivity, and support future growth by streamlining operations and integrating technology where appropriate.

- **Creating a Strong Team:** As your startup grows, you'll need to extend your team to handle the increasing workload and capitalize on new opportunities. Invest in hiring and retaining excellent talent, with an emphasis on people who share your startup's values and are dedicated to its long-term success.

- **Financial Planning and Management:** To support your growth plans, continuously analyze and adapt your financial estimates, budgets, and cash flow management procedures. This will allow you to keep control of your startup's finances, ensure you have the resources you need to seek new possibilities, and maintain financial stability as you grow.

Your startup will be well-positioned to scale sustainably and achieve long-term success if you set growth targets, focus on customer-centric strategies, diversify and expand, optimize operations, build a strong team, and maintain excellent financial management. Keep these techniques in mind as you go down the path to bootstrapped success to assist you handle the challenges and possibilities ahead.

Final Words of Encouragement

Dear Fellow Dreamer,

As we near the end of our adventure together, I'd like to say a few words of encouragement and inspiration. You've gone this far, and I'm confident that you have the ambition, determination, and enthusiasm to see your bootstrapped startup succeed.

Remember that the road to bootstrapped success is not easy or quick, but the pleasures and satisfaction that come from establishing a business from the ground up using your own skills and resources are genuinely priceless. As an entrepreneur, you have the ability to build something amazing and forge your own own path.

I've experienced personally the struggles and triumphs of bootstrapping a business, and I want you to know that you're not alone on this journey. Several entrepreneurs have gone before you, and their success stories demonstrate the power of perseverance, resourcefulness, and a tireless pursuit of one's objectives.

Thus, as you continue on this great journey, remember why you began in the first place. Maintain your enthusiasm, vision, and unflinching belief in yourself and your ideas. Maintain your concentration, stay diligent, and never stop learning and adjusting.

Accept setbacks, challenges, and unavoidable failures as chances for growth and learning. Make use of them as stepping stones to your ultimate aim. When you achieve your goals, remember to look back and appreciate how far you've come, understanding that every step, choice, and ounce of effort was worthwhile.

My final lesson to you is to be inspired, hungry, and to never give up on your entrepreneurial aspirations. One bootstrapped startup at a time, you have the potential to change the world. And I can't wait to see what amazing things you'll accomplish.

Here's to your self-made success!

Sincerely,

Nick Peret

AUTHOR BIO

~

Nick Peret is an accomplished entrepreneur with over 8 years of experience in the software and technology industries. His commitment to empowering businesses, combined with his keen eye for scalable strategies, has led him to co-found and scale two successful seven-figure technology startups. Better Boss Brands, Nick's most recent venture, focuses on optimizing sales processes and implementing effective systems for tech startups.

Nick's experience ranges from software implementation to CRM optimization, growth consulting, and lead generation. He also hosts the popular podcast Tech Startup Insights, where he imparts invaluable knowledge and advice to aspiring entrepreneurs.

Nick, an adventurer at heart, has traveled the world, from running marathons in New Zealand to living in Australia for six months and even skydiving in Hawaii. When he isn't pushing boundaries in his personal life, he devotes his time to assisting fellow entrepreneurs in their pursuit of success in the ever-changing world of technology and innovation.

Nick lives in Denver with his fiancee, Brittney, and their two dogs, Boss and Lambeau. To learn more about Nick's work and to get in touch with him, go to betterboss.io or follow him on social media.

- Website: betterboss.io
- Email: nick@betterboss.io
- LinkedIn: www.linkedin.com/in/nickperet

REFERENCES

∼

Resources & References

- Blank, S. (2013). The Four Steps to the Epiphany: Successful Strategies for Products That Win. K&S Ranch.

- Cardon, M. S., & Stevens, C. E. (2013). Managing Human Resources in Small Organizations: What Do We Know?. Human Resource Management Review, 23(2), 107-122.

- Croll, A., & Yoskovitz, B. (2013). Lean Analytics: Use Data to Build a Better Startup Faster. O'Reilly Media

- Dweck, C. S. (2006). Mindset: The New Psychology of Success. Random House.

- Feld, B., & Mendelson, J. (2012). Startup Communities: Building an Entrepreneurial Ecosystem in Your City. Wiley.

- Guillebeau, C. (2012). The $100 Startup: Reinvent the Way You Make a Living, Do What You Love, and Create a New Future. Crown Business.

- Halligan, B., & Shah, D. (2014). Inbound Marketing: Attract, Engage, and Delight Customers Online. Wiley.

- Holiday, R. (2014). Growth Hacker Marketing: A Primer on the Future of PR, Marketing, and Advertising. Portfolio/Penguin.

- Kawasaki, G., & Fitzpatrick, S. (2019). Wise Guy: Lessons from a Life. Penguin Publishing Group.

- Lencioni, P. (2002). The Five Dysfunctions of a Team: A Leadership Fable. Jossey-Bass.

- Maurya, A. (2012). Running Lean: Iterate from Plan A to a Plan That Works. O'Reilly Media.

- Metrick, A., & Yasuda, A. (2011). Venture Capital and the Finance of Innovation. Wiley.

- Mullins, J. (2014). The Customer-Funded Business: Start, Finance, or Grow Your Company with Your Customers' Cash. Wiley.

- Mullins, J. (2014). The New Business Road Test: What Entrepreneurs and Investors Should Do Before Launching a Lean Start-Up. Pearson.

- Nivi, B., & Ravikant, N. (2014). Venture Hacks: Good Advice for Bootstrapping Entrepreneurs. VentureHacks.

- Osterwalder, A., & Pigneur, Y. (2010). Business Model Generation: A Handbook for Visionaries, Game Changers, and Challengers. Wiley.

- Ries, E. (2011). The Lean Startup: How Today's Entrepreneurs Use Continuous Innovation to Create Radically Successful Businesses. Crown Business.

- Ries, E. (2017). The Startup Way: How Modern Companies Use Entrepreneurial Management to Transform Culture and Drive Long-Term Growth. Currency.

- Tuller, L. W. (2011). The Complete Idiot's Guide to Finance for Small Business. Alpha Books.

- Womack, J. P., & Jones, D. T. (2003). Lean Thinking: Banish Waste and Create Wealth in Your Corporation. Free Press.